Joyce Appleby on *Thomas Jefferson*
Louis Auchincloss on *Theodore Roosevelt*
Jean H. Baker on *James Buchanan*
H. W. Brands on *Woodrow Wilson*
Douglas Brinkley on *Gerald R. Ford*
Josiah Bunting III on *Ulysses S. Grant*
James MacGregor Burns and Susan Dunn on *George Washington*
Charles W. Calhoun on *Benjamin Harrison*
Gail Collins on *William Henry Harrison*
Robert Dallek on *Harry S. Truman*
John W. Dean on *Warren G. Harding*
John Patrick Diggins on *John Adams*
E. L. Doctorow on *Abraham Lincoln*
Elizabeth Drew on *Richard M. Nixon*
Annette Gordon-Reed on *Andrew Johnson*
Henry F. Graff on *Grover Cleveland*
David Greenberg on *Calvin Coolidge*
Gary Hart on *James Monroe*
Hendrik Hertzberg on *Jimmy Carter*
Roy Jenkins on *Franklin Delano Roosevelt*
Zachary Karabell on *Chester Alan Arthur*
Lewis H. Lapham on *William Howard Taft*
William E. Leuchtenburg on *Herbert Hoover*
Timothy Naftali on *George Bush*
Kevin Phillips on *William McKinley*
Robert V. Remini on *John Quincy Adams*
Ira M. Rutkow on *James A. Garfield*
John Seigenthaler on *James K. Polk*
Hans L. Trefousse on *Rutherford B. Hayes*
Tom Wicker on *Dwight D. Eisenhower*
Ted Widmer on *Martin Van Buren*
Sean Wilentz on *Andrew Jackson*
Garry Wills on *James Madison*

Inheriting the Revolution: The First Generation of Americans
Telling the Truth about History (with Lynn Hunt and Margaret Jacob)
Liberalism and Republicanism in the Historical Imagination
Capitalism and a New Social Order: The Republican Vision of the 1790s
Economic Thought and Ideology in Seventeenth-Century England
Jefferson: Political Writings (edited with Terence Ball)
Recollections of the Early Republic: Selected Autobiographies (editor)

Thomas Jefferson

Joyce Appleby

Thomas
Jefferson

THE AMERICAN PRESIDENTS

ARTHUR M. SCHLESINGER, JR., GENERAL EDITOR

Times Books

HENRY HOLT AND COMPANY, NEW YORK

Times Books
Henry Holt and Company, LLC
Publishers since 1866
175 Fifth Avenue
New York, New York 10010
www.henryholt.com

LIBRARY OF CONGRESS CATALOGING-IN-PUBLICATION DATA
Appleby, Joyce Oldham.
   Thomas Jefferson / Joyce Appleby ; Arthur M. Schlesinger, general editor.
     p.   cm.—(The American presidents)
Includes bibliographical references.
  ISBN-13: 978-0-8050-6924-2
  ISBN-10: 0-8050-6924-0
    1. Jefferson, Thomas, 1743–1826.   2. Presidents—United States—
Biography.   3. United States—Politics and government—1801–1809.
I. Schlesinger, Arthur Meier, 1917–   II. Title.   III. American presidents
series (Times Books (Firm))
E332 .A67 2003
973.4'6'092—dc21
[B]   200203563

First Edition 2003

Printed in the United States of America
3   5   7   9   10   8   6   4   2

FOR KAREN

who shares my love of history

Contents

Editor's Note

The president is the central player in the American political order. That would seem to contradict the intentions of the Founding Fathers. Remembering the horrid example of the British monarchy, they invented a separation of powers in order, as Justice Brandeis later put it, "to preclude the exercise of arbitrary power." Accordingly, they divided the government into three allegedly equal and coordinate branches—the executive, the legislative, and the judiciary.

But a system based on the tripartite separation of powers has an inherent tendency toward inertia and stalemate. One of the three branches must take the initiative if the system is to move. The executive branch alone is structurally capable of taking that initiative. The Founders must have sensed this when they accepted Alexander Hamilton's proposition in the Seventieth Federalist that "energy in the executive is a leading character in the definition of good government." They thus envisaged a strong president—but within an equally strong system of constitutional accountability. (The term *imperial presidency* arose in the 1970s to describe the situation when the balance between power and accountability is upset in favor of the executive.)

The American system of self-government thus comes to focus in the presidency—"the vital place of action in the system," as Woodrow Wilson put it. Henry Adams, himself the great-grandson and grandson of presidents as well as the most brilliant of American historians, said that the American president "resembles the commander of a ship at sea. He must have a helm to grasp, a course to steer, a port to seek." The men in the White House (thus far only men, alas) in steering their chosen courses have shaped our destiny as a nation.

Biography offers an easy education in American history, rendering the past more human, more vivid, more intimate, more accessible, more connected to ourselves. Biography reminds us that presidents are not supermen. They are human beings too, worrying about decisions, attending to wives and children, juggling balls in the air, and putting on their pants one leg at a time. Indeed, as Emerson contended, "There is properly no history; only biography."

Presidents serve us as inspirations, and they also serve us as warnings. They provide bad examples as well as good. The nation, the Supreme Court has said, has "no right to expect that it will always have wise and humane rulers, sincerely attached to the principles of the Constitution. Wicked men, ambitious of power, with hatred of liberty and contempt of law, may fill the place once occupied by Washington and Lincoln."

The men in the White House express the ideal and the values, the frailties and the flaws, of the voters who send them there. It is altogether natural that we should want to know more about the virtues and the vices of the fellows we have elected to govern us. As we know more about them, we will know more about ourselves. The French political philosopher Joseph de Maistre said, "Every nation has the government it deserves."

At the start of the twenty-first century, forty-two men have made it to the oval office. (George W. Bush is counted our forty-third president, because Grover Cleveland, who served nonconsecutive terms, is counted twice.) Of the parade of presidents, a dozen or so lead the polls periodically conducted by historians and political scientists. What makes a great president?

Great presidents possess, or are possessed by, a vision of an ideal America. Their passion, as they grasp the helm, is to set the ship of state on the right course toward the port they seek. Great presidents also have a deep psychic connection with the needs, anxieties, dreams of people. "I do not believe," said Wilson, "that any man can lead who does not act . . . under the impulse of a profound sympathy with those whom he leads—a sympathy which is insight—an insight which is of the heart rather than of the intellect."

"All of our great presidents," said Franklin D. Roosevelt, "were leaders of thought at a time when certain ideas in the life of the nation had to be clarified." So Washington incarnated the idea of federal union, Jefferson and Jackson the idea of democracy, Lincoln union and freedom, Cleveland rugged honesty. Theodore Roosevelt and Wilson, said FDR, were both "moral leaders, each in his own way and his own time, who used the presidency as a pulpit."

To succeed, presidents must not only have a port to seek but they must convince Congress and the electorate that it is a port worth seeking. Politics in a democracy is ultimately an educational process, an adventure in persuasion and consent. Every president stands in Theodore Roosevelt's bully pulpit.

The greatest presidents in the scholars' rankings, Washington, Lincoln, and Franklin Roosevelt, were leaders who confronted and overcame the republic's greatest crises. Crisis widens presidential opportunities for bold and imaginative action. But it does not guarantee presidential greatness. The crisis of secession did not spur Buchanan or the crisis of depression spur Hoover to creative leadership. Their inadequacies in the face of crisis allowed Lincoln and the second Roosevelt to show the difference individuals make to history. Still, even in the absence of first-order crisis, forceful and persuasive presidents—Jefferson, Jackson, Theodore Roosevelt, Ronald Reagan—are able to impose their own priorities on the country.

The diverse drama of the presidency offers a fascinating set of tales. Biographies of American presidents constitute a chronicle of wisdom and folly, nobility and pettiness, courage and cunning, forthrightness and deceit, quarrel and consensus. The turmoil perennially swirling around the White House illuminates the heart of the American democracy.

It is the aim of the American Presidents series to present the grand panorama of our chief executives in volumes compact enough for the busy reader, lucid enough for the student, authoritative enough for the scholar. Each volume offers a distillation of character and career. I hope that these lives will give readers some understanding of the pitfalls and potentialities of the presidency and also of the responsibilities of citizenship. Truman's famous sign—"The buck stops here"—tells only half the story. Citizens cannot escape the ultimate responsibility. It is in the voting booth, not on the presidential desk, that the buck finally stops.

—Arthur M. Schlesinger, Jr.

Thomas Jefferson

Preface

The United States in 1800 was a political phenomenon: an independent nation sprung from European colonies, a republic in a world of monarchies, a unique society resting on a broad base of property-owning family farmers. Enslaved men and women composed one fifth of its population (40 percent to 60 percent in Southern states), but that horrendous fact did not prevent America's leaders from speaking ardently of inalienable rights to justify their revolution. Independence brought self-government to the American states, but self-government was not the same as participatory democracy. That would require a more thorough transformation of American political culture. To accompany Thomas Jefferson through his presidency is to follow the tumultuous changes that turned the United States into a democratic nation, albeit one that tolerated slavery.

In leading America toward democracy, Jefferson also instilled the nation with his liberal convictions. That is, he succeeded in limiting the scope of government while protecting the informal public realm where people could form organizations, engage in politics, and freely trade with one another. So familiar to us are these elements of public life that we easily forget that it took a foresighted leader to pluck, from the quiver of America's possibilities, the two arrows of participatory politics and limited government.

Like the first decade of the twenty-first century, the first years of the nineteenth century found the world on the edge of a profound transformation. But, whereas globalization in our century has many advocates, in 1800 few people expressed belief in democracy. At the dawn of the new century, elitist attitudes prevailed in America. The spirit of equality animated some philosophers and reformers, but the people around them could scarcely fathom what egalitarian practices might involve. Most Americans—particularly the upper-class leaders of the Revolution—considered political independence their great triumph; they looked upon further social change as an invitation to the disorders they had already lived with during the protracted war with Great Britain.

According to conventional wisdom, the world was divided between the few and the many, the talented few who led and the ordinary many who labored. Privilege had a special, social bite. Plain men and women deferred to ladies and gentlemen when they entered a room or passed them on the road. Assumptions of superiority and inferiority lodged in children's minds and grew into the unexamined assumptions that silently supported adult attitudes. In European society, the vast majority of people were so poorly fed, so wretchedly dressed, that they seemed like a race apart. In the United States there really did exist a race apart—the enslaved men, women, and children, originally from Africa, who occupied the bottom rung of a social ladder not crafted for climbing.

In his conviction that America was destined to become a democracy, Jefferson differed from the cohort of leaders who had fought for American independence. They of course believed in freedom and made every effort to form governments that respected civil liberties and extended the suffrage. They admired the sturdy independence of the typical American man, which distinguished him from the middling sort in Europe, but they retained the respect for rank that dominated conventional thought. Jefferson alone among his American peers anticipated the age of democracy and bent every effort toward hastening its peaceful, consensual arrival.

Awareness of the deeply ingrained biases of a ranked society is essential to understanding what the democratic transformation of the United States involved. Jefferson is remembered as the author of the Declaration of Independence, an early advocate of religious freedom, and the purchaser of the Louisiana Territory, but his most unusual gift was that of political imagination. He resisted the notion that political equality was a chimera and strove to root out the last monarchical remnants from American culture. This work put him at odds with the country's privileged upper class and especially its political arm, the Federalist party.

To be sure, Jefferson sought political equality solely for ordinary white men and disguised that limitation in the rhetoric of universal rights. With respect to women and people of other races, he shared the prejudices of his peers. Jefferson's particular mix of traditional and unconventional affirmations accounts for his tenacious single-mindedness and his confusing ambivalences, his successes as well as his failures. Was he for universal rights? Was he against slavery? Did his racial prejudices undermine his reform program? Did his distorted picture of women prevent his being a democratic pathbreaker?

These questions about Jefferson passed seamlessly from nineteenth-century contemporaries to scholars to members of the public in the twenty-first century. Jefferson raised his voice against slavery on several important occasions, but he died convinced that whites and free blacks could never prosper together once slavery ended. He enjoyed the conversation of intelligent women, but taught his daughters that women were created for men's pleasure. He approached Native American culture with avid curiosity, but recommended the ruthless destruction of Indian ways. These repellent convictions jostled strangely with Jefferson's generous conception of the human potential. If they appall us, they should also provoke our wonder that anyone born in the bosom of a misogynist, slave-holding aristocracy could have dreamed of a society of equals.

Scholars are loath to credit a single individual with responsibility for momentous social changes. And they are correct. Most historical events have deep roots. The democratization of American society in the early nineteenth century is no exception. From the beginning of European settlement on the North American continent, it had been difficult to transplant government authority, social formalities, and economic regulations. American men, just because they had access to land, voted in larger numbers than anywhere else. The economic base of family farms and owner-run plantations nurtured independent ways. American prosperity promoted personal confidence and easy communication across class lines—the raw material for participatory politics. To these foundations for a democratic society Jefferson added rhetorical inspiration, political wisdom, and upper-class connections. As an insider, he saw the obstacles that elite prejudices and pretensions placed in the way of democratic practices. A highly ingenious leader, he was able to lay out a route around them.

Jefferson's vision accounts for the almost utopian zeal of his two administrations. They certainly explain his animus toward the Federalist party for installing a network of upper-class families to monopolize offices in the new constitutional order. By the time he became president, Jefferson had, for eight years, led a rambunctious political movement manned by thousands of white men eager to assert their right to be heard and esteemed. In opposing the Federalists, he ushered in a kind of sustained partisan activity that had never existed before. Initially called the Republican party, it became known in the era of Andrew Jackson as simply the Democracy; later on, it was called the Democratic party. But even the modern Republican party, formed in 1854, chose its name in part to honor Jefferson.

Thomas Jefferson remains the most controversial of the presidents of the United States because the contradictions in his ideals still affect Americans profoundly. They touch on natural rights, race, and the proper balance between liberty and equality in democratic rule. Jefferson sought change, innovation, novelty, but he was decidedly not a deracinated intellectual, writing incendiary tracts in a garret like Thomas Paine. Rather he was an insider, repeatedly elected to high office by his peers, the slave-owning planters of

Tidewater Virginia. It's safe to say that rarely if ever has a man with such a radical bent won so many elections from such an electorate. Solving this puzzle strains our historical imagination

Jefferson called his election America's Second Revolution, "as real a revolution in the principles of our government as that of 1776 was in its form." Inclined to treat this claim as a bit of victor's hyperbole, historians have not taken the pronouncement very seriously. This biography will. Two avenues of transformative change in Jefferson's presidency will get attention: his radical commitment to limiting government and his eradication of elite practices in the federal government. He was surely the first head of state who deliberately set out to narrow the scope of his and his successors' authority. And he succeeded, restraining the "energetic government" of his predecessors. He was also, and somewhat paradoxically, a self-conscious social engineer, using his discretionary powers to promote new, democratic manners for the United States.

Jefferson assumed power as an adversary. His inauguration climaxed a particularly rancorous election. Partisan campaigns had not been anticipated by the Founding Fathers fourteen years earlier. This was virgin political territory. Or to change the metaphor, President Jefferson had to reach office through a minefield. Once there, he transformed an amorphous opposition movement into a political party disciplined in governing. Once in office, Jefferson bent every effort to creating a liberal, democratic America. These historic developments form the interpretive matrix for this biography of America's third president.

1

A Pivotal Election

On March 4, 1801, a tall, narrow-shouldered man in his late fifties emerged from a boardinghouse in the capital city of the United States. He was heading for his inauguration as the country's third president. Disdaining the company of dignitaries or an honor guard, Thomas Jefferson walked with friends and supporters to the Capitol, where Chief Justice John Marshall administered the oath of office. Only a salute from a detachment of the Alexandria militia and the applause of the men and women gathered on the Capitol steps marked the special occasion. He had declined to wear even the ceremonial sword that John Adams had sported four years earlier. After thirty-five years in the public limelight, Jefferson was now to govern the nation according to ideas still deemed radical by almost half the voters. As he took office, the wounds from a searing presidential campaign and a cliffhanger of an electoral vote had not yet begun to heal.

Nor did the day start propitiously. The nation's second president had decamped earlier that morning in high dudgeon over his defeat, leaving Jefferson a curt note informing him that there were seven horses and two carriages in the White House stables. In the waning hours of his presidency, Adams had also appointed a slew of federal judges to dog his successor's days in the White House. Despite Jefferson's popularity with the voters, he now faced a thoroughly entrenched opposition in the Supreme Court and in a civil service honeycombed with Federalists.

Chief Justice Marshall was but the most conspicuous of the midnight judges. A Virginian like Jefferson, Marshall was no friend of the incoming administration. "Today . . . the new order of things begins," he had written that morning, adding ominously, "The democrats are divided into speculative theorists & absolute terrorists. With the latter I am not disposed to class Mr. Jefferson."[1] This was hardly the expression of confidence the new president needed after his election ordeal, but it was an honest response. The campaign had aroused fear and fury. Profound political disputes during the previous decade had rent asunder that collection of disinterested leaders the Founders had envisioned running the country.

When George Washington took office in 1789, few imagined that partisan disputes would disrupt the civic peace that the Constitution was designed to secure. The Federalist Papers, which explained the virtues of the Constitution, had actually banked on the formation of ad hoc majorities, not permanent ones organized to win elections. Neither did Jefferson nor James Madison imagine that they were jump-starting party politics when they went public with their concerns about the elitist cast of Washington's policies, though they certainly wanted to oust Federalists from office. Their cries of anguish about Alexander Hamilton's financial schemes and the administration's tilt toward Great Britain exposed the tip of an iceberg. Beneath lay profound differences dividing the old revolutionary leadership. Soon the electorate itself became polarized. The ill-fated Adams presidency unfolded under the shadow of partisan activity. Events knocked against each other like so many pool balls. The Alien and Sedition Acts, meant to rein in the routine invective found in newspaper columns, provoked the Virginia and Kentucky Resolutions; the quasi-war with France prompted the expansion of the army, which was followed by a taxpayers' revolt.

Federalists depicted a Jefferson so besotted with love for France that he would pervert America's most precious institutions to aid the French revolutionary cause. Republicans likewise wildly exaggerated the Federalist partiality to aristocratic rule. With so much at stake in the presidential election, dire warnings filled both the public realm and private letters. Virginia, Hamilton warned, would "resort to the employment of physical force" should Republicans lose. Writing his mother from Europe, John Quincy Adams passed along a French report "that the friends of liberty in the United States . . . [would] probably not wait for the next election, but in the mean time [would] destroy the fatal influence of the President and Senate by a Revolution." Other Federalists feared that the Jeffersonians planned a military takeover. Theodore Sedgwick and Fisher Ames predicted that the Republicans in the large mid-Atlantic states would attempt a coup once they had made their militia as formidable as possible. "It is obvious to me," Ames explained in early 1800, "that all other modes of decision will be spurned" as soon as the Republicans "think they have force on their side."

Republicans were no less alarmist, some even urging secession at the same time that they charged the Federalists with intending to introduce a monarchy or aristocracy before they had to yield power in March 1801. Because both parties had a strong regional basis, talk of disunion abounded in New England and the South. Both Federalists and Republicans expressed doubts that there would even be an election. Since the public had tolerated the detested Alien and Sedition Acts, Jefferson feared that the Federalists would pass "another act of Congress, declaring that the President shall continue in office during life." Referring to Hamilton as "our Bonaparte," he imagined a military intervention in support of Adams with a "transfer of the succession to his heirs, and the establishment of the Senate for life."[2]

By the time the election year rolled around (and the process did take a year, because the states chose their presidential electors in many different ways), the two parties assumed the worst about each other, and party discipline had replaced independent balloting. Party slates like that of Jefferson and Aaron Burr replaced lists of candidates from which electors chose victor and runner-up for president and vice president. When the actual voting ended, chimeras became real threats. Jefferson defeated Adams, but his electors had so loyally voted for both him and Burr that they produced a tie, catapulting the final choice into the House of Representatives that had been elected in 1798. There, a dozen devilishly partisan schemes hatched. The Constitution stipulated that when no one candidate had a majority, the names of the top five contenders be forwarded to the House. In this case there were only four contenders in all. "One state, one vote" was the constitutional rule, even though Delaware and Rhode Island had populations under 70,000 and Virginia contained close to 900,000 people. With only eight of the sixteen state delegations (Vermont, Tennessee, and Kentucky had now joined the union) firmly supporting Jefferson, there were not enough votes in the old House to elect him, but a sufficient number to drag out the balloting for nearly three weeks and thirty-five rounds of balloting.

The switch from the Electoral College turned Jefferson and Burr into competitors for the presidential plum. Since Burr was willing to play the spoiler, the Federalists had a field day voting on various combinations of Jefferson, Burr, Adams, and Charles Cotesworth Pinckney. They toyed with bizarre slates, even with the outrageous reversal of their standardbearers, Pinckney and Adams. Through round after round of balloting, representatives ignored the voters' intentions. Even the defeated president deplored the possibility that Burr—"this dexterous gentleman"—might become president: "What a discouragement to all virtuous exertion, and what an encouragement to party intrigue, and corruption!"[3] Most of the Federalists could not decide what they feared more: Jefferson's election or a revolutionary break with the new—hence fragile—constitutional government. Rumors of conspiracies and usurpations had been circulating since presidential voting began in the early fall. One contemporary characterized them as "uncommonly extravagant ravings."

War had again broken out in Europe. That and the raging political passions at home prompted dire conjectures about the fate of
the union. As so often happens at critical moments, someone found
the courage to act honorably. That someone in 1801 was James
Bayard, Delaware's sole representative and a Federalist, who deferred
to the will of the people by withholding his vote from Burr. Just
two weeks before the official inauguration day, March 4, the House
named Jefferson president-elect.[4] Three years later, Congress would
propose and the states ratify the Twelfth Amendment, separating
the ballots for president and vice president. Not men to shy away
from realities, America's political leaders recognized that parties
had come to stay.

After taking the oath of office, Jefferson delivered his presidential address in as inauspicious a manner as he had arrived at the
Capitol. No doubt relieved by the peacefulness of his inauguration,
he tried to douse the partisan flames that had burned fiercely and
unchecked for months. Ingeniously, he turned the vitriol of the
presidential campaign into proof of democratic vigor, describing it
as mere "animation of discussion" which would worry only "strangers
unused to think freely and to speak and to write what they think."
He then appealed to his fellow citizens to "restore to social intercourse that harmony and affection without which liberty and even
life itself are but dreary things," a sentiment that paved the way for
his famous declaration: "We are all Republicans—we are all Federalists." Emphasizing this point, Jefferson admonished his fellow
Americans to "bear in mind this sacred principle, that though the
will of the majority, is in all cases to prevail, that will, to be rightful,
must be reasonable; that the minority possess their equal rights,
which equal laws must protect, and to violate which would be oppression." He also warned the people against "entangling alliances,"
coining a phrase commonly attributed to George Washington. At
the completion of the inaugural address, the crowd dispersed, and
Jefferson returned to his lodging, where he took a place among his
fellow boarders at the noon dinner table.

Among those in attendance that morning was Margaret Bayard Smith, who accompanied her husband to Washington, where he became editor of the principal newspaper and she wrote novels and sketches of life in the capital. Born into a Federalist family, she soon became Jefferson's strongest advocate. In a description of the Capitol, she wrote that it was guarded by venerable oaks. "Beyond the Capitol-Hill as far as the eye could reach, the city, as it was called, lay in a state of nature," she continued, "covered with forest trees, fields of grain, and verdant plains with here and there a house." It was a view that no doubt stirred appreciation in Jefferson who wanted to return the government to a pristine state.

Writing after his victory to the English scientist Joseph Priestley, who was then ensconced in rural Pennsylvania, Jefferson succinctly reprised the differences between the Democratic-Republicans and their Federalist opponents—who, he wrote, had looked "backwards not forwards, for improvement." The Federalists favored education, Jefferson acknowledged, "but it was to be the education of our ancestors," and he noted ruefully that President Adams had actually told audiences that "we were never to expect to go beyond them in real science." Rising to this handsome occasion for expatiating on the future, Jefferson declared with great gusto: "[W]e can no longer say there is nothing new under the sun. For this whole chapter in the history of man is new. The great extent of our republic is new. Its sparse habitation is new. The mighty wave of public opinion which has rolled over it is new." "The mighty wave of public opinion" was something of an exaggeration, for Jefferson had won the election with only seventy-three electoral votes to Adams's sixty-five.

Thirty-three years earlier, Jefferson's talents and social position had won him a seat in colonial Virginia's House of Burgesses. Soon events beyond his control turned him into a rebel, a lawmaker, and a statesman. Tall, red-haired, a fine horseman and gifted musician, Jefferson had mastered the classics, mathematics, horticulture, architecture, and natural philosophy by the time he took his seat at twenty-five. A lawyer and a planter, he shone more for his intellectual gifts than his political ones. His father, who had died when he was four-teen, represented an American archetype, the man who goes to the frontier to build for himself what other slaveholding planters inher-ited. His mother brought him connections to the world of inherited wealth through membership in the all-powerful Randolph clan. Neither parent can account for Jefferson's brilliance, his way with words, or the expensive tastes that kept him in debt. Nor can they have been responsible for that unique political vision that has left Americans in his debt.

The signaling, singling hand of reputation tapped Jefferson for prominence when his "Summary View of the Rights of British America" joined the polemics of the American resistance move-ment in 1774. The British colonies were far gone along the road to revolution by that year. When Jefferson joined the Second Conti-nental Congress meeting in Philadelphia in May 1775, the dele-gates were teetering on the verge of rebellion. He and John Adams homed in on each other like talent-seeking missiles. Adams consid-ered Jefferson his protégé, but deferred to his gifts as a writer when it came time for the drafting committee to come up with a document explaining why the colonies intended to declare their independence.

Jefferson was thirty-three in that glorious year of independence, 1776, and his personal life was in shambles. His mother's death in the spring had precipitated a crippling bout of migraine headaches that confined him to his bed for weeks. His much-loved wife, Martha Wayles Skelton, suffered from successive pregnancies. In their first year together, Martha was born; from five subsequent births, two more daughters survived. In 1782 came the blow that Jefferson had struggled so hard to avert: his wife died, never having fully recov-ered from her last pregnancy, the seventh in ten years of marriage. Martha Jefferson reported her father's terrible grief in her journal; for his part, Jefferson, a fanatic record-keeper, burned all of the cor-respondence between him and his wife.

During these years, Jefferson stayed as close to his home as pos-sible. Serving on the committee to revise the laws of now independ-ent Virginia, he worked on them in his study at Monticello. His position as an ambivalent reformer became evident at once. He dreamed of expanding the suffrage for white men and gaining religious tolerance for Virginia's many sectarians, but he wrote laws that failed to moderate the state's draconian slave code.

In 1780, in the midst of his prolonged season of grieving, Jefferson became governor of Virginia. It was not a good time. The War for Independence had turned nasty in 1779 when the British moved south and dropped the conciliatory policy that had marked their engagement with the Continental Army in New England and the middle states. With their archenemy, France, pouring money and men into the American cause, the British finally took off the velvet glove and invaded the South with ruthless intensity. Governor Jefferson failed to rally the Virginia militia to meet the new threat and found himself the personal target of an audacious raid. Fleeing on horseback with the state's official papers in his saddlebags, he barely escaped capture. Charges of cowardice followed, not entirely erased by a legislative inquiry that cleared his name.

In 1783 the Virginia legislature sent Jefferson to the Continental Congress. His work there on the ordinances for the Northwest Territory reinforced his reputation as a master craftsman in lawmaking. The following year, Congress sent him to France as America's representative.

Jefferson in Paris was a man intoxicated with ideas, with conversation, with traveling, with playing a hand in the great diplomatic game of Europe. He became particularly fascinated with the possibility of replacing the tacit consent of the governed with a genuine, explicit endorsement of current laws. "The earth belongs in usufruct to the living," he wrote Madison. Then, taking the proposition quite literally, he set about calculating the optimal space of years between appeals to the electorate if each generation were to hold its own plebiscite on the body of laws ruling their lives. Making the point quite sharply, he declared that "the rights of one generation will scarcely be considered hereafter as depending on the paper transactions of another."

These ruminations give the first evidence of Jefferson's running battle with the past. Everywhere he looked, he saw habits, customs, prejudices, veneration of the past obliterating the potential of the new, laying the heavy hand of tradition on youthful exuberance. In language he found the deadening force of tradition as well. If existing laws constrained each cohort of the living, how much more profoundly inhibiting was the conceptual vocabulary babies acquired through language. He saw that in learning to talk, human beings took in a particular way of thinking. Dilating on two words he had just learned—*purism* and *neologism*—Jefferson announced that he was "not a friend to what is called purism, but a jealous one to the neology which has introduced these two new words into our dictionary without any authority." Writing with his usual confident elegance, he continued, "I consider purism as destroying the verve and beauty of the language while neology improves both and adds to its copiousness." Demoting dictionaries, he called them "but the depositories of words already legitimated by usage," while society became "the workshop in which new ones are elaborated." The very concept *society*—a coherent group of people conceptually different from family, church, and state—was novel when he wrote those words.

In Paris, Jefferson was again thrown together with John Adams, this time with the added zest of Abigail Adams's company. Their friendship ripened as they worked together negotiating loans and treaties. Adams and Jefferson were strange collaborators, as future events were to disclose. Adams's famous flintiness kept him from chasing chimeras. It also blocked his awareness of the genuine changes going on around him. Democracy held no charm for Adams. Ordinary men were, to him, just that: ordinary. His head was full of awe and admiration for history's great statesmen and thinkers. When aristocracy fell into disrepute in the early nineteenth century, he mourned its loss. A true conservative, Adams looked to the ancients for wisdom and expected the world to go on pretty much as it had for millennia.

Jefferson was, if anything, anticlassical. He declined to venerate ancient wisdom. His expectation of inexorable improvement undercut the importance of past knowledge, an attitude nicely epitomized when he wrote that the introduction of representative democracy "has rendered useless almost everything written before on the structure of government." And then, delivering the coup de grâce to classical learning, Jefferson added that this fact "in a great measure relieves our regret if the political writings of Aristotle, or of any other antient, have been lost." Radical in the sense of wishing to pull out by the roots the traditions that constrained men and frustrated progress, Jefferson was willing to entertain almost any new idea.

The United States enjoyed a remarkable continuity of leadership as the men who came to prominence during the Revolution passed smoothly into the principal offices in the Confederation and soon the new constitutional order. They discovered their political differences when the unexpected happened. For Jefferson and Adams, the arrival in 1787 of the draft Constitution, reported out of the Philadelphia convention, was one. Both men were still on diplomatic missions in Europe, far from the fascinating developments taking place at home. The opinions they then exchanged foreshadowed the political divisions in the United States for the next three decades. The Constitution's provisions for the presidency drew their immediate attention. Despite his calling the convention "an assembly of demi-Gods," Jefferson characterized the new executive as "a bad edition of a Polish king" (Polish rulers were elected for life). Adams didn't like the presidency for different reasons. He went right to the heart of his differences with Jefferson when he responded: "You are apprehensive the President when once chosen, will be chosen again and again as long as he lives. So much the better as it appears to me."[5] He added a line that vibrated with alarm: "Elections, my dear sir, Elections to offices which are great objects of Ambition, I look at with terror."[6] This sentiment must have given Jefferson a start. He never referred to it in subsequent letters, and soon both men were on their way home, Jefferson to join George Washington's cabinet as secretary of state, Adams as the first vice president elected under the new constitution. Had the three of them listened more carefully to one another during these months abroad, when every day's mail brought news of a startling development, they might not have been caught off guard when Jefferson mounted an opposition against the elitist tendencies of Washington's administration four years later.

The unanticipated outbreak of the revolution in France fired Jefferson's political imagination; it also coincided with the organization of Washington's administration in faraway New York. As leaders in the United States formed a new government with calm deliberation, French radicals rushed to dismantle the old regime with breakneck speed. Jefferson, still in Paris as American minister, followed with rapt attention the storming of the Bastille and the episode of the Tennis Court Oath, when members of France's Third Estate pledged one another to stay in session until they had produced a constitution for France. The abolition of feudal privileges and the adoption of the Declaration of the Rights of Man and the Citizen deeply impressed him. As he wrote in his autobiography, "[M]y conscientious devotion to these rights could not be heightened, but it had been aroused and excited by daily exercise." Then breathlessly he catalogued the abuses being addressed: "the cruelty of the criminal code generally, the atrocities of the Rack, the venality of judges and their partialities to the rich; the Monopoly of Military honors by the *Noblesse*; the enormous expenses of the Queen, the princes & the Court; the prodigalities of pensions; & the riches, luxury, indolence & immorality of the clergy." With rhetorical brio, Jefferson concluded that "surely under such a mass of misrule and oppression, a people might justly press for a thoro' reformation, and might even dismount their rough-shod riders, & leave them to walk on their own legs." Anything seemed possible that heady summer of '89 when Paris was "still in high fermentation." As Jefferson was packing up to return in the fall, a crowd of market women stormed Versailles and brought the king and queen back to the city, where they could be observed. Thirty-nine months later those same crowds would gather to watch heads roll upon the guillotine during the Reign of Terror.

Paradoxically, while the French were busy destroying their old authoritarian institutions, the Americans seemed busy creating new ones. Fresh from the most radical milieu in the Old World, Jefferson landed in one of the most conservative in the New, or at least so it appeared to him as he became acquainted with his fellow cabinet members. An elegant social life had sprung into being during the sessions of the first Congress held in New York. "Here, certainly, I found a state of things which, of all I had ever contemplated, I the least Expected," Jefferson confided in his notes, going on to explain that he had left France "in the first year of her revolution, in the fervor of natural rights, and zeal for reformation." When he was quickly included in a round of dinner parties, he learned that the members of Washington's cabinet and most legislators there gathered did not share his political enthusiasms. "I cannot describe the wonder and mortification with which the table conversations filled me," he reported, adding dejectedly that "a preference of kingly over republican government was evidently the favorite sentiment," and that he found himself "the only defender of republican government unless there chance to be some like-minded Congressmen present."[7] In these months Jefferson came to view the men in Washington's administration as a dangerous faction that had been welded into a mighty political machine by Alexander Hamilton.

For many, the round of presidential levees, balls, and dinners signaled the consolidation of a national elite ready to exercise as much authority over matters of taste as over national policies. The lavish entertaining that dismayed Jefferson seemed aimed at creating a virtual aristocracy to intimidate ordinary Americans just as real aristocrats awed the impoverished masses of Europe. Instead of finding colleagues as thrilled as he was at the fall of absolutism in France, Jefferson encountered officials at best indifferent to the revolutionary potential of the 1790s. Members of Washington's official family and Federalist congressmen railed at the disorderly tendencies of ordinary men and congratulated themselves at having saved the American experiment in self-government from a dangerous slide toward democracy. Like the French conservatives, they looked to

Britain's constitutional monarchy for guidance in the difficult task of balancing liberty and order.

The aristocratic tone of Washington's administration might have remained just a worrisome tendency to Jefferson had not the fiscal policies of the treasury secretary, Alexander Hamilton, given substance to his fears that the new government was intentionally blunting the reforming thrust of the American Revolution. A bold innovator, Hamilton put together a package of brilliantly conceived laws designed to turn the nation's sizable revolutionary debt into an asset. These laws triggered a round of unseemly speculation in government bonds, very much benefiting those wealthy investors in the know. Highly sensitive to the corrupting influence of such financial wizardry, Jefferson saw a hydra-headed monster taking shape at the heart of the new government. It would be hard to imagine two men more unlike than Jefferson and Hamilton, though each grudgingly recognized the other's integrity. At base, Jefferson didn't understand commercial economy very well, but far from humbling him, this deficiency confirmed his opinion that Hamilton was up to no good.

When he looked back on this period twenty-five years later, Jefferson was still convinced that Hamilton had adroitly played on the self-interest of a "mercenary phalanx" to make himself master of Congress. Disappointed in the structure of the new government, Jefferson thought that Hamilton had maneuvered his way around the separation of powers to control Congress from his place in the executive branch, turning the government toward the parliamentary system of Britain. In Jefferson's eyes, only the organization of an opposition meant "to preserve the legislature pure and independent of the executive" could save the country from Hamilton's minions. Giving himself the part of a latter-day St. Patrick, Jefferson was only too happy to drive the snakes from the capital.

Hamilton had been dead fourteen years when Jefferson revisited his notes on the 1790s. Then he recalled him as "a singular character. Of acumen outstanding, disinterested, honest, and honorable in all transactions, amiable in society, and duly valuing virtue in private life, yet so bewitched and perverted by the British example, as to be under thorough conviction that corruption was essential to the government of a nation." To rule the country as treasury secretary required a feeble president, and Jefferson so described Washington, whose "memory was already sensibly impaired by age, the firm tone of mind for which he had been remarkable, was beginning to relax, its energy was abated, a listlessness of labor, a desire for tranquility had crept on him, and a willingness to let others act, and even think for him."[8]

Increasingly, Jefferson felt isolated from both the people and the policies of Washington's cabinet. Unwilling to stifle his fears, he reached out to the public. Far from being a usual thing to do, this act signaled the beginning of political parties. The conventional wisdom held that officeholders, though duly elected or appointed by elected officials, conducted their business in private, going to the voters for approval or disapproval only at election time. Rousseau had dismissively asserted that the English people were free only one day in seven years—the day when they were allowed to vote. His remark reminds us of the difference in eighteenth-century thinking and our own. While we consider voting rights and political participation one and the same thing, two hundred years ago they were separated.

To appeal to voters outside of elections was to give them a political role they had never had before. In looking outside the capital for those who shared his anxiety, Jefferson got a boost from events in the French Revolution. In January 1793, it took a violent turn with the execution of Louis XVI. The American public suddenly took notice: their old ally, France, had declared itself a republic. As unexpected as the news from France, a fresh group of American radicals appeared on the political scene. These new political participants rallied to the Gallic call for "liberty, equality, and fraternity" while stunned Federalists denounced the French Republic as the work of dangerous zealots. With Madison as his principal ally, Jefferson tapped into this exuberance, mounting a campaign to change the direction of the government by cultivating a critical stance toward the Federalists, in preparation for voting them out of office.

Fast on the heels of news of the death of the French monarch came Edmond-Charles-Edouard Genet, the extravagant Citizen Genet, first emissary from the French Republic to the Republic of the United States. Bound for Philadelphia, where the American government resided during preparation of the District of Columbia, Genet actually landed in Charleston, South Carolina, whence he swept up the Eastern Seaboard on the tide of a spectacular outburst of popular acclaim. Banquets, bonfires, parades, and liberty poles marked his passage from town to town. In the wake of Citizen Genet's northward movement, these exuberant supporters of France created an informal political network of clubs and newspapers, an utterly new phenomenon in America. They boldly imitated the notorious Jacobins of the Reign of Terror. The Democratic Society of Philadelphia, for instance, resolved to measure time from the day of Independence, and its secretary duly dated minutes "in the eighteenth year of American Independence." Civic feasts were held. Members called one another "citizen," and they devoted long evening meetings to drafting statements about Washington's policies.[9]

From the Federalists' point of view, widespread white male suffrage was laudable exactly as long as the common people deferred to the political wisdom of their superiors. It was precisely the removal of crucial areas of national governance from vulgar majorities in the individual states that demonstrated the superior features of the new U.S. Constitution. An elite leadership, filtered by successive screens for talent, probity, and virtue, would reclaim America's political institutions from the excesses of wartime democracy. The decorum, formality, even secretiveness of the Washington administration embodied the political mores of the American gentry, who deliberately distanced themselves from those who simply voted. To inspire awe was considered essential to the capacity to rule. The great desideratum of the Federalists, led by Washington and Hamilton, was to restore the dignity of government after the disruptions of revolution and to attach the rich and well-born firmly to the fledgling institutions of the new nation. From such a perspective,

Jefferson's willingness to lead the young radicals who had taken to the streets seemed pure madness.

All that was socially transformative about the American Revolution was still a potentiality, waiting for these electrifying shocks to bring it to the surface. In the earlier debates over the ratification of the Constitution, the Anti-Federalists had argued that freedom and civic virtue could flourish only in a small, self-governing republic, but the Federalists had prevailed with their bolder plan for a modern, centralized, extended republic. After ratification, the two sides had quickly composed their differences. What neither side in that debate of 1787–1788 had imagined was that the new government would actually generate a dynamic political movement unbounded by state loyalties and fueled by popular passions, themselves fanned by events abroad.

Recovering the sense of surprise with which America's national leaders responded to each other in 1793 puts into perspective the exaggerated fears and ugly accusations that marked the birth of America's first political parties. This surprise, in turn, promoted mutual anger and outrage in men who had worked together through the long years of resistance, revolution, and constitution-writing. Most of them had met when the separate protests against Great Britain turned into a united rebellion in 1774 and 1775. After that, they served in Congress or the army or returned home to govern their now independent states. United by the enormous task of securing independence, they had had little chance to discover areas where they might disagree.

Wishing to keep the United States out of the European war that had erupted again, President Washington announced a policy of neutrality. This decision, prudent though it was, enraged those who had formed a passionate attachment to the cause of the French republic. Swiftly, what had begun as a spontaneous effusion of sympathy for a fellow republic turned into a fight over American foreign policy. Announcing their convictions at tumultuous public gatherings, these new entrants into American politics aroused the worst fears of the Federalists. No issue, domestic or diplomatic, escaped the ferocious opposition the Republicans put up to Federalist rule.

Angry denunciations of the policies of Washington's administration, now charged with being slavishly pro-British, accompanied demonstrations of support for the French Revolution. The country was enjoying a period of great commercial expansion—itself a consequence of the profits American merchants earned as neutral carriers for the warring countries of Europe. Prosperity promoted the construction of roads, the extension of postal services, and the founding of local party newspapers. This communication network vastly enhanced the reach of the raucous public criticism encircling the Federalists.

What began as differences over neutrality and treaty-making soon turned into a grand debate about free speech and popular political participation. Earlier, Adams had confessed, "There is nothing I dread so much as a division of the Republic into two great parties." When parties developed during his second term as vice president, he charged that the "turbulent maneuvers" of partisans "tie the hands and destroy the influence" of those desirous of the public good. The Federalists maintained that after voting, citizens should let their elected officials govern, while the Jeffersonians articulated a political philosophy that took popular sovereignty literally, insisting on the people's right to engage in vigorous politicking. Gathering in taverns and coffeehouses, America's new citizens avidly read the papers and, armed with a little information, threw themselves into intense debates about public policy. Such assertions of involvement in day-to-day political issues challenged venerable notions about how ordinary voters should behave. Both the British and the colonial American governments had witnessed tumults, but these had been interpreted as aberration, not as an intrinsic part of self-government. Now young men, intoxicated by events in France, were organizing into clubs where they spent their evenings issuing high-sounding resolutions.

In the early debates of the French General Assembly, disputants crafted two models of political order. To the British example of sober, ordered constitutional government committed to securing as much personal freedom as the flawed nature of human beings could handle, they opposed the American vision of social harmony arising naturally from freedom-loving men's cooperative capacities. Americans returned the favor during Washington's second term by juxtaposing revolutionary France, leading the world to a bright democratic future, against steady Great Britain, with its civil liberties, unwritten constitution, and social hierarchies. The pro-French Jeffersonians reinterpreted America's revolution as a rejection of the past. Both sides, as John Marshall's comment on inauguration morning suggests, exaggerated their differences, ratcheting up the stakes until all decency, good sense, and future hope appeared at risk, at least rhetorically.

Not even Washington's enormous prestige could summon the people back to the recognition that they should leave the responsibility for governing to their leaders. Believing that the Western Pennsylvania Democratic Club had encouraged armed resistance to the whiskey tax, Washington used his annual address to Congress in 1794 to call for the disbanding of what he dismissively called "self-created societies." His effort boomeranged. Club members took his remarks as proof that the government intended to silence them. What else was the United States, one opposition writer countered, but "a great self-created society"?

During these contentious years, the positions of power in the executive branch of the United States were held by men who were socially conservative and intellectually unadventurous. They drew their truths from a kind of secular Calvinism, an amalgam of wisdom drawn from the classics and the Bible: men and women are prone to sin, and society is subject to degenerative diseases. The specialness of the United States lay not in its signaling a new dispensation for the human race, but in its offering enlightened statesmen an opportunity to apply the lessons of the past. According to these national leaders, when the American colonies separated from Great Britain, they freed themselves from the mother country's corruption, not its political example. Their history taught that order preceded and conditioned liberty and that gentlemen chosen by discerning citizens could alone preserve that order. These Federalists, true sons of England, extolled personal freedom—it was the most cherished element of their heritage—but they distinguished readily between liberty and license.

John Adams defeated Jefferson handily in 1796, the expectation that the vice president would naturally succeed the president carrying him into office. He followed faithfully in Washington's big footsteps, retaining the first president's cabinet and pursuing his policy of neutrality. Having faced what seemed to him unseemly opposition, Adams entered the presidency distracted and harassed. He was not a man to bear criticism easily, and his political convictions persuaded him that boisterous popular political participation was wholly unwarranted. As for Jefferson, his comments to friends indicate that he expected to triumph next time. Taking the high ground of impartial generalizations, he observed to his good friend John Taylor that party divisions were probably necessary "to induce each to watch and relate to the people the proceedings of the others." Such optimism would be tested during the Adams years.

Lacking Washington's heroic stature and calm dignity, Adams had a vexed presidency from the beginning. European warfare continued to imperil the new nation. Both the French and the English preyed on the country's shipping, raising the risk, but not diminishing the ardor, of American merchants for their profits. Like a small terrier scurrying between two fighting mastiffs, the United States pursued its commerce recklessly while struggling diplomatically to gain some relief from foreign depredations.

The terrier is not a bad metaphor for President Adams, who had hardly taken office when the French refused to receive an American ambassador. Watching the Federalists defer to Great Britain, successive French governments had come to see the United States as more hostile than neutral. The new French ruling body, the Directory, announced further that it would seize any American ships carrying British goods. Aroused by this bellicose gesture, Adams urged Congress to prepare for war, while at the same time he sent three

American commissioners to Paris to plead for peace. Instead of opening negotiations, the Directory sought compensation from the United States for its pro-British acts. Made informally, the request seemed like solicitation of a bribe—a humiliating bribe. News of the insult from Messrs. X, Y, and Z, as they were called in published documents, threw the American public into a frenzy. Robert Goodloe Harper won the hearts of fellow Federalists when he toasted Adams with "Millions for Defense, but not one cent for Tribute." It became the slogan of the hour, and the Federalists briefly tasted the sweetness of public favor.

In their moment of sudden popularity, the Federalists in Congress passed the Alien and Sedition Acts, fulfilling the Jeffersonians' long-standing predictions that the government would try to silence them. The public disapproval of the Republicans that arose from their pro-French sympathies dissolved in the acid of outrage over the new measures. Republicans and Federalists agreed that newspapers could influence public opinion and that public opinion could be a powerful force in a self-governing country. They differed in how they valued these truths. Republicans counted on a free press to carry their criticisms of the Adams administration. For the Federalists who looked upon themselves as the government more than a party, the implications of these ugly facts were clear: those newspapers given over to wild and incendiary attacks on the government must be closed. As dispensers of government patronage since 1789, the Federalists had managed to discourage all but the most determined (and often flamboyant) Republican publishers. In fact, Federalist or apolitical newspapers outnumbered Republican papers three to one.

Under the Sedition Act, zealous Federalists prosecuted every major Republican newspaper publisher. More than a dozen persons were tried for criticizing the government, and the newly refurbished army harassed both editors and protesters. Matthew Lyon, who had actually been elected to Congress by editing a fiery Republican journal, became an early target of prosecution. Federalist judges even printed their decisions in pamphlets designed to explain why good order demanded the swift muzzling of Republican rags. Aliens—particularly radical French and Irish émigrés who had gravitated to Jefferson's orbit—were threatened with deportation, though only one was actually deported.

Federalist jingoism accompanied the military preparations, which trebled the size of the army, established a navy, and unleashed U.S. privateers on French ships. Adams, struggling with dissension within his own party, seemed curiously out of touch with the people, who resented the suppression of their political activity and loathed the new taxes levied to pay for the military buildup. Jefferson, presiding over the Senate as vice president, sought refuge from Federalist vindictiveness at Monticello, where he counseled even more greatly overwrought Republicans against secession. He advised "a little patience": "we shall see the reign of witches pass over, their spells dissolved, and the people recovering their true sight, restoring their government to its true principles." In the event, he was correct, but his patience did not prevent him from working with Madison to get the Virginia and Kentucky legislatures to pass resolutions condemning the Alien and Sedition Acts as unconstitutional.

In 1799, Adams sent another mission to France and successfully ended America's quasi-war with its first ally. Often considered a heroic act, Adams's overture can also be seen as expedient. It followed the news that public opinion had shifted away from the Federalists. The voters of Pennsylvania, a bellwether state, decisively elected a slate of Republican officials, indicating that the country had soured on Federalist prosecutions and wearied of a president who lost few opportunities for lecturing men, women, and children on their duties. Even more fascinating, the Sedition Act failed to stanch the flow of Republican bile; rather, it politicized a host of printers, who rushed to found newspapers during the election year of 1800. When the votes for president were counted in December, Jefferson had won seventy-three electors to Adams's sixty-five.

Rarely do presidential elections produce a mandate, but the sharpness of the differences between the Republicans and the Federalists gave Jefferson's victory a decisive quality. The two parties had squared off on the issues of foreign policy and revolutionary hopes, on free speech and the permissible bounds of popular politics, on whether to use the Constitution to limit or energize the federal government. Escalating the stakes, the Jeffersonians said that they were fighting to ensure that America would truly be the "last, best hope of the world," as the French philosophe Anne-Robert Turgot had called it, rather than fading into a pale New World imitation of Great Britain.

That the campaign of 1800 was one of the most acrimonious in the annals of American history is true, but the statement views the election through the wrong end of the telescope. Looking backward, the 1800 election can be compared with those of 1828, 1864, 1896, or 1932, but looking forward from 1800 the vituperation was unprecedented. Washington had become president as the unsullied hero of Valley Forge and Yorktown. Six years later, a dozen opposition newspapers had sprung into existence for the express purpose of sullying that reputation. Men who had once been comrades in arms crossed the street rather than exchange civilities. Even those who had campaigned together for the ratification of the Constitution—like Hamilton and Madison, who together wrote the Federalist Papers—became adversaries five years later. Marshall's description of Republicans as "absolute terrorists" or "speculative theorists" reveals the hypercharged environment. That such a clear-thinking man would entertain such fears of a fellow Virginian, Jefferson, who had been in public service for thirty-three years, shows that the disputes of the 1790s cut deeper than contests for power or disagreements over policy. These men were fighting over the meaning of the revolution and, by extension, of America itself.

Years later, when Adams and Jefferson resumed a correspondence, Jefferson summed up in self-congratulatory terms their differences in pairs: the guidance of experience or of theory; fear and distrust of the people as opposed to "cherishment" of them; use of coercive power versus trust in the people's capacity to act in their best interests.

His was the party of theory, democracy, and restrained authority. But it was not the champion of enslaved men and women. That distinction belongs to the Federalists, many of whom joined the antislavery societies forming in the 1780s and 1790s. Hostile to democracy, they cared deeply about freedom, and their Northern base permitted them to be outspoken on an issue that deeply perplexed Southerners. None of the Virginia statesmen who led the nation—Washington, Jefferson, Madison, Monroe, Marshall—expressed more than the conventional late-eighteenth-century educated view that slavery was evil and should eventually be ended.

Jefferson's election to the presidency lifted the curtain on one of the most passionate and dramatic political struggles in American history. Washington and Franklin were now dead; Adams was rusticating in rural Massachusetts. A cadre of distinguished leaders, young men during the Revolution, now directed the country's affairs. Their ambitions mingled with motives worthy of classical heroes who fought wars and founded nations. Hamilton, Burr, Marshall, Madison, John Randolph, James Monroe, and, of course, Jefferson now moved into the last act of the American Revolution, the one that would disclose the character of the society brought into being in 1776.

Most Americans now naturally side with the Jeffersonians because it was they who foresaw what the nation was to become. Their democratic ambitions became the country's guiding principles. No political party would arise again claiming that ordinary voters needed the guidance of the rich, well-born, and well-educated. Nor would many American politicians in the future claim "the guidance of theory" as a virtue, as Jefferson had. The Federalists misjudged American voters and their likely acquiescence to a ruling elite. In retrospect, the Federalists seem almost more radical in trying to impose the ideals of European aristocracy upon the reality of Americans' robust independence. Still, the Jeffersonians surely misjudged the voters as well, for in the long run the American electorate has shown little tolerance for continued revolution at home or abroad. What they evidently wanted they got: a leader who believed in their capacity to govern themselves and would liberate ordinary white men from the thrall of their social superiors.

2

Defining His Presidency

Two weeks after his inauguration, Jefferson moved into the White House. Congress would not convene until December, so he had nine months to enjoy the bucolic charms of Washington. John Adams might well have cast an envious look at the breather fate had given his successor, for Jefferson had plenty of time to put his executive house in order. Even the warring powers in Europe calmed down, ending eight years of hostilities in October, though this proved to be more of a time-out than a lasting peace. The new president proceeded to outrage the Federalists with his appointments and his assault on formality, while he thrilled his party with his consensus-building skills.

As leader of an opposition, Jefferson had to appoint a totally new cabinet, at the same time filling the myriad of lesser jobs in customs bureaus and post offices. And he wanted to do it in the Republican style evoked by his party when they asked voters to reject the Federalists. That is, the federal government would be open to talent, rather than being the preserve of distinguished families. He had also promised to cut the size of government. At the same time Jefferson had to provide protection and support to a rapidly growing country. American families were streaming across the Appalachian Mountains to claim land in the West. The center of population in the United States steadily moved away from the Atlantic seaboard. The migration gave concrete proof of the country's continental ambitions, despite the disconcerting presence of France, Spain, and Great Britain in the Mississippi Valley. In responding to this array of challenges, Thomas Jefferson defined his presidency by setting a new direction for the country and the century.

Nothing could be further from the truth than the claim by John Adams's great-grandson, the historian Henry Adams, that once Jefferson took office he outfederalized the Federalists. The thrust of Adams's shaft, which has lodged itself in our history textbooks, was that, having run on a platform of limited government, Jefferson expanded federal powers with the Louisiana Purchase in 1803 and the national shipping embargo in 1806–1807. Adams's assertion errs in both directions: in misconceiving the profundity of Jefferson's reforms and in assuming that the Louisiana Purchase and the embargo are measures more Federalist than Republican.

The thoroughness with which Jefferson exorcised the influence of his predecessors still astounds. He released from imprisonment all who had been convicted of sedition by issuing an executive order ending all prosecutions under the Alien and Sedition Acts and letting the acts lapse. In 1802, Congress dropped the waiting period for becoming a United States citizen from fourteen years to five. Jefferson's campaign had promised simplicity, economy, and an end to elite rule. He delivered on these pledges; he removed a whole cohort of young Federalists from civil and military offices, eliminated domestic taxes, reduced the national debt, and shrank the size of the civil service—all this despite a growing population and the doubling of the country's territory during his years in office. He also hastened the conveyance of land in the national domain to ordinary farmers. Still further, Jefferson gave the ship of state, to use his words, "a republican tack" by banishing Federalist formality from presidential appearances, receptions, and dinners.

Not a symbol, a civil servant, or a presidential initiative escaped Jefferson's consideration as a tool for dismantling the Federalists' "energetic" government. And after his two terms, Jefferson had the exceptional good fortune to see his policies continued by two close friends, James Madison and James Monroe. This "Virginia dynasty" lasted a quarter of a century, long enough to embed Jeffersonian values in American institutions for the entire antebellum period. The Virginia presidents imbued their successors with their under-standing of the proper relation between federal and state authority, an understanding that lasted until the question of slavery rent the union and opened Americans to a new exercise of federal power.

The first president to be inaugurated in the District of Colum-bia, Jefferson could take justifiable pride in Washington City's very existence. Initially, the up-and-coming port of New York had served as the nation's capital. The fastest-growing urban area in the United States, New York embodied America's future, but its polyglot pop-ulation and rough neighborhoods seemed at odds with the coun-try's overwhelmingly rural character. Many Americans feared the piling up of people in cities. They didn't fancy urban sophistication either. Jefferson shared their qualms. In 1790, he shrewdly took advantage of a crisis to wrest from Secretary of the Treasury Alexan-der Hamilton a promise to move the capital. He next persuaded Virginia's congressmen to vote for Hamilton's fiscal program in return for a measure to create a ten-mile-square site for a new capi-tal city on the Potomac River. Pennsylvania legislators got the capi-tal moved to Philadelphia while the new city was being readied.

Next to George Washington, whose death prompted the name change from Federal City to Washington City, Jefferson cared most about the new capital. Pierre L'Enfant, who had come to America from France to fight in the Revolution, had laid out a magnificent plan for Washington that revealed the influence of the royal palace at Versailles. L'Enfant conceived of a great city with wide boulevards radiating from hubs adorned with commanding statues. An amateur architect himself, Jefferson arrived in the District of Columbia with L'Enfant's grand design in his head. This was good, for everything visible about the place was raw and unfinished in March 1801. L'Enfant's boulevards existed only on paper. The president had to dip into his own pocket to buy Lombardy poplars to line the one public avenue, the unfinished gravel road joining the president's office to Capitol Hill. To secure an income for William Thornton, who was supervising the completion of the Capitol, he named Thornton to the post of superintendent of patents.

With some 3,500 permanent residents, the embryonic metropolis looked more like a village. Washington's skyline, if such a word can be employed, plummeted from the vaulting dome on Capitol Hill to the modest two-story structures around it. One could see unfinished buildings in every direction, some under construction, others abandoned after funds ran out. Speculators had jacked up the price of real estate, discouraging investors. A shortage of capital and faith slowed the city's progress. While the new president worked on ways to finance the completion of the public buildings, others plotted to abandon the idea of a new capital city altogether. When Jefferson finally got Congress to appropriate enough money to finish the south wing of the Capitol, he appointed Benjamin Latrobe surveyor of U.S. public buildings. Generally considered America's first architect, Latrobe was also an engineer and an innovator in public works and architectural style. Jefferson greatly admired Latrobe's Greek Revival designs and became his most important patron. Both of them paid for their mutual admiration by incurring the displeasure of Thornton, who had won the original competition for the Capitol's design a decade earlier.

Nothing quite captures the competing pulls of Jefferson's enthusiasms as well as the capital city itself. Jefferson, the economizer in government, was at war with Jefferson, the designer and collector of objects of beauty and curiosity. During his second term, he oversaw the addition of the two arcaded wings that still grace the White House. He probably would have rejected the notion that there was a contradiction in his character, by pointing to the difference between private and public spending. He wanted the federal government to be open, frugal, unpretentious, and agreeable to ordinary men and women, but he apparently felt no dissonance between such a goal and his own love of attractive, useful, and comfortable objects. It took more than forty pieces of luggage, including bulky crates, to bring back to the United States the wine, books, musical instruments, art objects, and carriage equipment he had acquired during five years in Paris.[1]

Although John and Abigail Adams had moved to Washington the preceding winter, the possibility of Jefferson's election had discouraged members of Adams's staff from settling there permanently. Margaret Bayard Smith, the lively chronicler of the city's first four decades, aptly described their situation:

> Like a flock of birds of passage, they only, as it were, alighted on the ground, and with their leader, the ex-President, took flight early on the fourth of March. Owing to these peculiar circumstances the city on that day lost half of its migratory population, and its wide surface had a desert and solitary appearance.[2]

No streets, no mass of houses proclaimed a city here. Just one wing of the Capitol had been built; the House of Representatives met in a room temporarily fitted up to accommodate them.

The President's House, as it was then called, had twenty-three rooms. Abigail Adams said that it would take thirty servants to staff it properly. Jefferson, for whom decorating a house amounted to a passion, quickly assembled the elegant furnishings that would be his silent companions for the next eight years. Having made economy the watchword of his administration, he himself bore the costs of outfitting his domestic space. He could afford to do this because the presidential salary of $25,000 a year was princely at a time when manual laborers earned some $300 a year. Having been convinced of the need for thrift, Republican congressmen tightened the purse strings, waiting to see if Jefferson instituted his vaunted economies before they appropriated more money for public buildings in Washington. He did, and they released more funds.

The Federalists, believing their own outlandish claims about Jefferson's character and habits, had talked themselves into a high pitch of anxiety as power shifted to the Republicans that fateful

March. Well aware of the agitated state of public opinion, Jefferson composed an inaugural address designed to smooth the ruffled feathers of the opposing flock. It soothed, but also led astray. Federalist listeners interpreted Jefferson's inaugural statement—"We are all Republicans; we are all Federalists"—to mean that there would be no purging of Adams appointees. Here they were disappointed, because Jefferson removed many Federalists from office; but also disappointed were the victorious Republicans who expected their man to wash the malevolent Federalist spirit out of national office altogether.

Almost every president has found making appointments an irksome task, but Jefferson had the extra burden of organizing the first opposition government. He had to reward the stalwarts who brought him into office, but he had to do so without totally deranging the governmental apparatus already in place. Less high-mindedly, Jefferson's supporters panted for lucrative posts: collectors of the ports, for example, received handsome fees. Jefferson tried to steer a moderate course, but he failed to satisfy his most ardent backers, and he certainly did not escape Federalist scorn.

Having sponsored the Constitution and controlled the government under it for its first twelve years, the Federalists saw themselves as The Government. Washington began his presidency with the conviction that he presided over the nation as a whole. He fitted the best men to the right office and then governed from a consensus. This policy looked disinterested until critics emerged with an attack on the elitist tendencies of his regime. Federalist officeholders under Washington and Adams stubbornly resisted the Republican charge that they were beneficiaries of party patronage. From their perspective, the first presidents had quite appropriately appointed the best men they could find. Even after their defeat in 1800, the Federalists had difficulty adjusting to the fact that they had lost office because they had lost a legitimate election.

Jefferson's attitude was a bit subtler. He wanted to achieve a better balance than the total incumbency of Federalist holdovers would allow. By his count, there were 316 offices whose incumbents he could appoint or remove. These did not include military or judicial offices for which there were established appointment processes. Waiting for Federalist officeholders to die, he reasoned, was too slow; resignations were infrequent, and malfeasance would be rare. So he outlined a policy of removals based on misconduct or egregiously partisan behavior. All vacancies would be filled with Republicans. Jefferson further complicated these broad guidelines by refusing to honor the appointments made by Adams during the lame duck period between his December defeat and Jefferson's inauguration three months later. These were the so-called midnight appointments, and there were a lot of them. Nothing rankled Jefferson quite as much; as he reminded Abigail Adams years later, those appointed "were from among my most ardent political enemies from whom no faithful cooperation could ever be expected." Jefferson also let it be known that—unlike Adams, who rewarded his own and other Federalist officials' family members—he would not give jobs to even distant relatives. Juggling a sense of rectitude with a desire to staff his administration with men guided by republican principles, Jefferson struggled with the triple challenge of defending the citizenry from punitive Federalist officeholders; strengthening the party he headed; and being his own man.

Another factor complicated the situation. The number of officeholders had grown as a consequence of Hamilton's state-building. Jefferson had no taste for bureaucracy, but if he cut down the number of civil offices too drastically, no vacancies would be left for Republican aspirants, and Federalist influence in the lower echelons of government might last his whole term. In the end, his dislike of extravagant government won out: he abolished what he regarded as a "multitude of useless offices" which, to his way of thinking, opened doors to fraud and embezzlement. Although Jefferson is hailed as the founder of West Point, he took his usual parsimonious course: as created in 1802, the institution was an underfunded band of twenty engineers, hardly the military academy that Alexander Hamilton had plumped for earlier.

No one challenged Jefferson's right to pick his own cabinet

officers, and this he did quickly, in the two-week interval between his election and the adjournment of Congress. The old Senate, still sitting, approved James Madison's nomination as secretary of state; Henry Dearborn's as secretary of war; and Levi Lincoln's as attorney general. Together with Albert Gallatin, who received a recess appointment, these men began to function as a cabinet in May. Robert Smith joined the group in July as secretary of the navy. Only Vice President Aaron Burr was excluded from the Republican harmony Jefferson orchestrated, his behavior during the tense weeks of balloting in February having made him almost persona non grata.

Jefferson chose Meriwether Lewis as his private secretary. Lewis, a distant cousin, lived with Jefferson in the President's House, remarking to a friend that they were like two mice in a church. Two years later, Jefferson's two sons-in-law, who had both been elected to Congress, moved into the upstairs of the White House. Though they added a familial note to the bachelor tone of the establishment, John Wayles Eppes and Thomas Mann Randolph were also sources of concern for their father-in-law. Neither man had a distinguished political career, and Randolph's hypersensitivity prompted him to move out for a spell, after he became convinced that his father-in-law preferred Eppes to him.

In keeping with the consultative style of government Jefferson was about to pioneer, he did not make his removal policy final until he had discussed it with his cabinet. The Federalists' unwillingness to see themselves as a mere party—and a minority one at that—had a great deal to do with the outrage they expressed when Jefferson actually removed some of them from office. Howls of derision greeted his decision to replace all the midnight appointments, and his published explanations failed to diminish Federalist ire. One leader, with snobbish disdain, predicted that Jefferson would not nominate any man who would be admitted into decent New England parlors. There was a sting of truth in this venomous remark, but the arrogance of the Federalist elite had politicized a whole generation of ordinary voters—men unacceptable in decent parlors—as subsequent elections were to demonstrate. These "mushroom candidates," as the Federalists derisively called them, formed the enlarged pool from which Jefferson picked his officeholders.

There were few distinguished Republicans outside the contingent of Southern planters, although Treasury Secretary Gallatin came from a prominent Swiss family. The Republican party simply did not have the abundance of educated, well-connected men that the Federalists could call upon. Jefferson's followers were more typically new men—younger, from less prominent families, thrown into public notice because of their opposition to the Federalist establishment. In choosing among them, Jefferson insisted on local approval and general respectability, but personal ability went further with the new president than wealth and social position. All of this was to be expected after a presidential campaign that excoriated social stratification and urged average voters to develop political skills.

Americans did not naturally turn to political careers. They preferred private occupations. The competing allure of starting a business or moving west greatly increased the difficulty Secretary Gallatin had staffing the Treasury, the largest department in the government. At one point, frustrated in his effort to fill less remunerative positions, he even suggested naming women to certain posts, a proposal that elicited Jefferson's curt reply: "The appointment of a woman to office is an innovation for which the public is not prepared, nor am I." Gallatin had inadvertently probed the limits of Jefferson's capacity to imagine a totally new order.

The Federalists' sense of entitlement went deep. They believed that the Constitution had succeeded in pulling the country back from the dangerous leveling experiments of the 1780s. When Jefferson pressed forward with plans to make government more accessible, he assaulted the Federalist conviction that good order required everyone to stay in his or her proper place. Deaf to the appeal of egalitarian values, Federalists attributed bad motives to the president's democratic gestures. Adding to their spleen were the laments of disappointed applicants. Although he beseeched Gallatin "to get us relieved from this horrible drudgery of refusal," Jefferson maintained a dignified silence in the face of criticism. "My usage," he wrote his friend Benjamin Rush, "is to make the best appointment my information and judgment enable me to do and then fold myself up in the mantle of conscience and abide, unmoved, the peltings of the storm."

In the years after Adams's defeat, political recriminations intensified. Fierce partisanship accompanied the democratization of politics in the nation. Partisan malice reached beyond party affairs. The Yale science professor Benjamin Silliman, reflecting on the behavior of his friends when talk turned to politics, described them as "ravenous wolves" despite their "most amiable and gentle disposition" in private life. Alexander Hamilton's son James recalled that the partisan hostility destroyed all social intercourse between the leaders of the different parties. More personally, William Henry Harrison and Joseph Story, as young Republicans, lost sweethearts to the Federalist prejudices of the women's families.[3]

Jefferson's appointment policy, despite all its compromises and temporizing, strengthened the Republican party. The crucible of politics burned off old notions of disinterested gentlemanly rule and left Jefferson with an opposition movement turning into a national party. The Federalists fulminated about retaliation at the polls, but the tide was running in the opposite direction. Their tendency to lash out at everything Jefferson did left them resembling the boy who cried wolf. And they deplored Jefferson's actions in such hyperbolic terms that he had little incentive to mollify them. His decision to give up attempts at conciliation no doubt contributed to his landslide reelection in 1804.

No two-term president in American history had a more stable cabinet than Thomas Jefferson. Only the attorney general changed; that post's final incumbent, Caesar Rodney, gave some indication of why Jefferson enjoyed harmony with his six department heads when he described to his father with obvious delight the president's "open, undisguised frankness to his official advisers whether when singly or in cabinet meeting or council." Early in his term, Jefferson set the tone for relations with his cabinet by inviting help both individual and collective. Gallatin and Smith, for instance, produced lengthy critical commentary on the draft of his first address to Congress. Far from intimidating those around him, Jefferson elicited candor, tapping into the kind of experience needed to govern wisely. Not infrequently, the cogent reasoning of a cabinet member could deflect him from a course of action. As he once commented, in cabinet meetings his vote counted as one. (Rarely, though, did the cabinet conclude business with a vote. More normally, an informal consensus prevailed—not without occasional heated debate.)

Typical of Jefferson's dependence upon consultation was his seeking advice from all on foreign relations. Each man had his brief, but all were relied upon for their advice on executive policies, presidential addresses, and how best to get along with the states and with other nations. An exceptional record-keeper, Jefferson kept track of the details of governing, but he also let his officers run their departments. Nor did he seem to flinch when they responded as tartly as Gallatin once did when he wrote the president, "I am in toto against this recommendation." Rather than hold weekly meetings, Jefferson would summon his six principal advisers when an issue demanded their attention. Often too they stayed for dinner, set at three-thirty. A cabinet member who had been called individually to the White House in the morning would leave in time for Jefferson to take his daily horseback ride through Washington's wooded paths. The president's was an orderly life.

When Congress convened in December, Jefferson won the approval of his Republican fellows by eschewing the pomp of a formal appearance. His concerted effort to shed the forms and pretensions of his Federalist predecessors had begun. Drawing on his years presiding over the Senate as vice president, Jefferson prepared a manual of parliamentary procedures for the new Senate, a surprising undertaking were it not so typical of the pains he took with public matters. Breaking with Federalist precedent, Jefferson sent his annual address to Congress in written form instead of delivering it in person. The address itself had gone through many revisions, with the cabinet members deliberating over the drafts. The news of most consequence came from the far-off Mediterranean, where the pasha of Tripoli, irritated by American parsimony in the matter of payoffs for the safe plying of the waters of North Africa, had declared war on the United States. Jefferson wanted congressional approval for having a naval squadron sent into the Mediterranean.

Jefferson's hard line with the pasha protracted hostilities for another four years, but bellicosity and patience paid off. A peace treaty signed in June 1805 brought to an end the four-year war with the Barbary pirates. The American navy had performed admirably, particularly when Commodore Edward Preble swept into Tripoli and set fire to an American frigate that had been captured. Horatio Nelson called Preble's raid "the most bold and daring act of the age"—hyperbole, no doubt, but hyperbole sweet to the ears of Americans, whose shoestring military operations always carried the risk of public humiliation. The American navy successfully maintained a blockade of Tripoli, and the pasha finally agreed to a mere $60,000 ransom for the three hundred captured sailors from the frigate, who had heard him proclaim that, having killed his own father and brother, he would not scruple to dispatch a few infidels. Jefferson deflected attention from the ransom by handsomely declaring that in a "government bottomed on the will of all, the life and liberty of every individual citizen become interesting to all."[4]

Closer to Jefferson's heart when he was first reporting to Congress in 1801 was the announcement that the government could now safely dispense with all internal taxes, including excises, stamps, auctions, and licenses. Happy, too, were data from the 1800 census showing that America had a population of more than five million. "Agriculture, manufactures, commerce, and navigation": these Jefferson named as "the four pillars of our prosperity," adding that they were "the most thriving when left most free to individual enterprise." The written form of his annual messages to Congress served him well: the press that had burgeoned in the hothouse of contested elections gave them good coverage. Republican leaders in the states often had them published as pamphlets. Through the annual messages, the public heard the good news that taxes were going down along with government expenditures.[5]

Jefferson's relations with Congress became as smooth as those with his cabinet. This was not all that surprising, considering that the 1800 elections had returned sixty-seven Republicans, while the Federalists held thirty-nine House seats. The size of the next Congress reflected the increases from the 1800 census, with a House of 141 seats, Republicans garnering 102, or 72 percent of the total. (It was this Congress, the Eighth, to which Virginia sent both of Jefferson's sons-in-law.) The Senate was equally skewed, with twenty-five Republicans to nine Federalists, leaving only four states securely in the Federalist camp. Small wonder that Jefferson never had to veto a piece of legislation.

The 1800 census also registered the fact that nine of the original thirteen states had started their long proportional decline as Western states joined the union. Only New York, New Jersey, and Georgia continued to outpace the national growth. Virginia still sent the largest delegation, with twenty-two representatives, a perverse total: white slaveholders benefited from counting their slaves, though each counted as only 3/5 of a man. Next came Pennsylvania, with eighteen, and New York and Massachusetts, with seventeen. Ten years later New York would overtake Virginia, but the rapid peopling of the frontier already foreshadowed the decreasing voting strength of the thirteen original states. In New Jersey, women who were single and held property voted until 1807, when all women were barred from voting. (They were far from being indifferent to politics: one woman delayed her marriage until after an election.)

Jefferson had written in 1798 that the Republicans preferred to rely on the legislature, as being the more democratic branch of the government. Yet rarely has Congress supported a president so comprehensively as did the Seventh, Eighth, Ninth, and Tenth. True to his principles, Jefferson worked closely with Republican congressmen, treating them with a respect that made him a consummate party leader. Evidently a believer that there is no limit to the good that you can do if you don't care who gets the credit, Jefferson kept a low presidential profile. Offering a striking contrast to Adams's frenzied conduct in office, Jefferson's composure reassured his staff and supporters. He confined expressions of irritation to personal conversations and letters to close friends.

As it turned out, the refurbishing of the White House had a political dimension, for Jefferson gathered senators and representatives at his dinner table almost daily when Congress was in session. Federalists, too, got invitations, but unabating party warfare soon made it prudent to confine them to separate evenings. Representative Samuel Latham Mitchell, who came to Washington from a flourishing New York medical practice, declared Jefferson "more deeply versed in human nature and human learning than almost the whole tribe of his opponents and revilers." To those revilers, Jefferson's mounting popularity was an affront. It outraged their sense of justice—and sometimes their sense of good taste, as when they learned that the farmers of western Massachusetts had decided to make the world's largest cheese to present to their president. Weighing in at 1,235 pounds, the offering arrived in time for New Year's Day, 1802, accompanied by a proud boast: "The Greatest Cheese in America, for the Greatest Man in America."

Keeping up the hospitality he was famous for at Monticello, Jefferson delighted his guests with the quality of food and drink, not to mention the lively talk that a man with his omnivorous curiosity could stimulate. Like a power hostess, he kept track of who had sat at his table, checking off the names of his guests against a congressional roster. While twelve was the favored number, dinner parties might include from eight to fifteen people. When Congress was in session, representatives and senators dominated the guest list. Frank about the political intent of these parties, the president explained to a correspondent that he created opportunities to avoid the jealousies and suspicions that could be "injurious to the public interest." He also fêted cabinet members, Supreme Court justices, foreign dignitaries, and their wives.

Jefferson was known abroad, particularly in France, for his enlightened enthusiasms and liberal views. When the young Baron Alexander von Humboldt finished his five-year exploration of Latin America, he came to Washington to share the scientific fruits of his remarkable trip with the president and cabinet. Speaking Spanish, French, English, and German—sometimes all in the same anecdote—Humboldt astounded and delighted the guests at Jefferson's table as much as he did his host. One visitor, the playwright William Dunlap, left a charming account of the president. Describing him as tall and thin, with hair worn in "negligent disorder," Dunlap told how Jefferson conversed with ease and vivacity, "possessing true politeness, which places his guests perfectly at their ease . . . he talked of the early approach of spring, of gardening French & English, preferring the latter & prais[ing] their great taste in laying out their ground."[6]

It's doubtful that Jefferson's dinner parties ameliorated the degree of partisanship in Congress, but the evenings did confront Federalists with a host whose elegance and erudition belied their charges of malevolence. Even John Adams acknowledged his charm, writing that one "never can be an hour in this man's company without something of the marvellous." During one 110-day period when Congress was in session, Jefferson recorded forty-seven dinners for 153 different men and women, half of whom dined twice. In the spring of 1804, he tallied up his entertainment outlay and found that 651 people had dined at his table since the first of December. He also noted that they had consumed 207 bottles of champagne. Calculating that one bottle served three and half persons, Jefferson put in a generous order for forty cases for the coming year. He noted the earliest and latest dates that his favorite vegetables were available in the city markets for the eight years that he kept a table there. Before the days of refrigeration, he could serve raspberries for only one week, broccoli for two, artichokes for six, and lima beans for three. Tomatoes could be enjoyed for almost four months.[7]

When Jefferson spoke of "a republican tack," he sought to distinguish his party from the Federalists with respect to their preoccupation with rank and status. Democracy, he realized, was as much about social habits as political beliefs. A genuine reform of society would demand changes in behavior as urgently as new convictions.

Rather than lecture his people into progressive practices, Jefferson set in motion a variety of convention-shattering initiatives, based on the assumption that the body had to change what it did before the brain could imagine different ways of thinking. Formality he viewed as the handmaiden of hierarchy. The presumption of social superiority that upper-class men and women conveyed in dress, carriage, voice, and gesture operated automatically; breaking with ingrained ways of thought and behavior would require a direct assault.

Jefferson began with a radical revision of White House etiquette. Deriding what he called "the rags of royalty," he turned modesty—of person, place, and ceremony—into an important feature of his administration. The contrast with his predecessors was stark. Hamilton had advised Washington to be accessible only to department heads, foreign ministers, and U.S. senators. The Federalists idealized a president who was a remote dignitary shielded by protocol. To inspire awe was to elicit deference from ordinary voters, to convince them subtly that governing was beyond their ken.

Jefferson banished protocol, that system of formalities carefully calibrated to reflect the relative importance of dignitaries at official gatherings. Jefferson preferred pell-mell to protocol. He refused to follow the rules for honoring foreign dignitaries. At his parties, he who was standing nearest the dining room door when the meal was announced went in first. He even chose a round table for his dinners to avoid arraying his guests in any semblance of ranked order. During the day, the president was quite capable of answering the front door of the White House if he happened to be walking by, even if dressed in his lounging robe. He abandoned the levees and receptions of the Washington and Adams eras, celebrating only the New Year and July Fourth, and those with open houses. With the White House doors thrown open, residents of the district could commemorate the day with the author of the Declaration of Independence. Jefferson's first public reception was exemplary: one hundred guests, including a delegation of Cherokee chiefs, gathered to celebrate the nation's fifteenth anniversary, the only birthday Jefferson said he ever remembered. Not exactly the city's whole population, the gathering was inclusive enough to please Republicans. Although the Marine Band normally played at such occasions, Jefferson, allowing his ear for music to get the better of his commitment to simplicity, imported some Italian musicians for the Fourth in 1805.

By removing the customary props to a structure of ranks and degrees, Jefferson hoped to weaken the entire edifice of existing hierarchies of family, government, and religion. Nor was he reluctant to articulate the political implications of his confrontations with the arbiters of polite society. Writing anonymously in the Philadelphia *Aurora*, Jefferson announced that since March 4, 1801, there had been no "Court of the United States." "That day," he declared, "buried levees, birthdays, royal parades, processions with white wands, and the arrogance of precedence in society, by certain self-styled friends of order, but truly styled friends of privileged orders." Jefferson had flushed out the political messages in formality, and he wanted Republicans to know it. Making men and women aware of their actions broke through the sense of naturalness that always gives force to habit.

As one diplomat noted, the president was "careful in every particular of his personal conduct to inculcate upon the people his attachment to a republican simplicity of manners and his unwillingness to admit the smallest distinction, that may separate him from the mass of his fellow citizens." Jefferson, he went on to say, received visitors at any time of day "with a most perfect disregard to ceremony both in his dress and manners." Far from indicating thoughtlessness or negligence on the president's part, Jefferson's reforms of etiquette had been carefully considered. They provided the contrast with the Federalists that he wished to sharpen; they embodied the republican simplicity that he had extolled in his presidential campaign. Even his personal habits affronted Federalists. For instance, in his daily horseback rides, Jefferson rode unaccompanied by a servant. Such indifference to genteel mores disgusted the New Hampshire senator William Plumer, who fumed in his diary that the president's appearance was so at variance with the practices of gentlemen that it "ill accords with the dignity of the Chief of a great nation."

The grand climax to Jefferson's campaign to bring simplicity to the federal government came in 1803 with the arrival of Anthony Merry, Great Britain's first minister to the United States. At the time, Washington was still largely rural despite the many construction sites. The Merrys contributed to the urbanizing effort by devising an imposing residence remodeled from two existing houses. Accompanied by a parade of white servants carrying an endless succession of crates, boxes, and trunks, the Merrys made a grand entrance. Their arrival alerted the denizens of the capital city that their social avatars had arrived.

On November 28, Madison in his capacity as secretary of state brought the new ambassador to the White House for his formal presentation to the president. Merry wore full diplomatic regalia: a coat trimmed in black velvet and gold braid, a plumed hat, handsomely buckled shoes, and that European mark of high status, a sword. The president, disconcertingly, was nowhere to be found when they arrived. Minutes elapsed while Madison searched for him through the downstairs rooms of the White House. When Jefferson finally emerged from his study through a side door, his attire horrified Merry. The president, he later reported, was not merely in a state of undress, but "actually standing in slippers down at the heels," his "pantaloons, coat, and under-clothes indicative of utter slovenliness and indifference to appearances and in a state of negligence actually studied." We have to give Merry credit for that last observation—"in a state of negligence actually studied": as he discerned, the president's outfit had been well thought out.

Merry, who had established diplomatic procedures on his side, protested his treatment vigorously. And there were further breaches of etiquette to aggravate the wound, including Jefferson's failure to honor prevailing forms and lead Mrs. Merry in to a state dinner. Madison, speaking for the new administration, pointedly told Merry that he could no more demand social distinctions in the United States than an American emissary could ask for equality with royals at the Court of St. James's. Never mollified, the Merrys finally refused to accept invitations to White House functions altogether. While some at the time attributed Jefferson's dismissive reception of Merry to his well-known anglophobia, it was entirely in keeping with the informality he had cultivated from the outset. Jefferson used the citizenry's critical view of elite rule to initiate new forms of White House etiquette that accorded ambassadors and average visitors equal respect. He hoped that these new manners would instill self-respect and obliterate deference in the same stroke. When he invited Merry to dine alone with him and the Spanish minister, Merry demurred, on grounds that he wanted to consult his government. Even Jefferson disliked being snubbed. "It is unheard of that a foreign minister has need of the permission of his court to sit down at the table of the head of state," he wrote indignantly, adding sarcastically, "I shall be highly honored when the King of England is good enough to let Mr. Merry come and eat my soup."[8]

Like any dabbler in human nature, Jefferson understood others to the extent that he understood himself. Indeed, one gets the strong impression from Jefferson's writings that he sought to release the Thomas Jefferson in every man. Bristling with more curiosity than he had time to satiate, Jefferson directed his social engineering to liberation. While virtue and responsibility were the civic ideals of the Federalists, he responded more rapturously to the freedom to explore, to express, to think, to travel, and to form opinions. And he feared that the dead hand of the past inhibited all of these freedoms. Sensing that the Federalists were trying to elevate the new Constitution to some empyrean realm, Jefferson ridiculed those who looked upon constitutions with "sanctimonious reverence and deemed them like the Ark of the Covenant too sacred to be touched." In countries "left free," he predicted, the forms of social existence would be emergent and fluid. Without set practices, sacred constitutions, and inhibiting authorities, experience itself would furnish men and women with the material for making decisions. Liberated once and for all would be man the doer, the inventor, the adapter, the improver—*Homo faber*—the universal man hidden from himself by tyrants, priests, and overlords. One can see in all these expectations the source of Jefferson's enduring appeal, for his were the values that continue to flourish in the United States today.

One can not help but wonder where the capacity to act on these iconoclastic ways came from, considering how conciliatory and soft-spoken Jefferson was. He was aided in this campaign by a striking indifference to being thought provincial. Much of the presidential formality of Washington and Adams—Washington's elaborate receptions, Adams's frettings over finding the proper way to address officials—can be attributed to their longing to appear correct in European eyes. Jefferson appeared unfazed by such concerns. He seemed to glory in his abandonment of ostentation and enjoyed the negligence about forms and dress that so affronted Federalist sensibilities. His statement in the *Aurora* article that "certain self-styled friends of order" who prescribed formality for the government were truly "friends of privileged orders" represented a genuine conviction.

Jefferson also eschewed his generation's obsession with honor. Dueling in the United States throve on political warfare. Unprepared for the give-and-take of partisan disputes, America's first politicians were its first duelers. Introduced into the United States by European officers who came to fight with the Continental Army, dueling acquired a peculiarly American twist. Where in Europe duels were mainly confined to military officers who quarreled about gambling debts and women, Americans dueled over politics. In the early decades of the nineteenth century, political opponents were quick to challenge one another to a duel if they thought that their honor had been sullied.

Helpless to change the elitism of the elite, Jefferson sought instead to limit their power. Once in office, he dismantled as much of the Federalist armature for a vigorous, central government as was practical. He cut taxes, reduced the size of the civil service, and let centralizing laws lapse. Here the irony of unintended consequences enters in. His efforts to contract the size of government shrank the overall importance of government, directing attention away from the polity and toward the economy, where everyone—including women, adolescents, the propertyless and enslaved—had a place.

While Jefferson certainly never sought an enlarged public role for either women or African Americans, his campaign to level hierarchies worked in diverse ways to hasten their civic recognition. Like the ordinary men whose cause he did champion, women, immigrants, and free blacks found in the expanded commerce of the early republic openings to a larger world. For women, in particular, the popularization of politics brought them unprecedented scope for action, despite rhetoric that idealized their domestic lives. In dozens of new ways, they were able to give the lie to assertions about their incapacity to participate in the public realm.

It was not at all clear even in 1801 what the Declaration of Independence had done by saying that "all men are created equal and endowed by their creator with certain inalienable rights among which are life, liberty and the pursuit of happiness." Most of the revolutionary elite saw few radical implications in this affirmation of natural rights. They expected continued deference; they supported the authority of patriarchal families, established churches, and legitimate governments. American independence for them appeared as a codicil to their grand English inheritance of freedom under the law.

Jefferson espied something different: the possibility of freeing (white) men from constricting institutions. He saw ordinary folk as so many Gullivers tied down by a hundred strings of custom and command. As he wrote to James Madison in 1787, "I owne I am not a friend to very energetic government. It is always oppressive. . . . [I]t is my principle that the will of the Majority should always prevail." It soon became evident, to the horror of many a Federalist, that Jefferson wanted to dismantle the old social order so that men so long alienated from their true natures might recover them. Against the prevailing view that people were weak, unsteady, in need of guidance, Jefferson built a political program on the Enlightenment faith in the rational, self-improving, independent individual who could be counted on to take care of himself and his family provided that intrusive institutions did not interfere. His remark to his much admired philosophical friend Pierre-Samuel Du Pont

refines his attitude: "We both consider the people as our children, &
love them with parental affection. But you love them as infants
whom you are afraid to trust without nurses; and I as adults whom I
freely leave to self-government."[9] Jefferson assumed an innate
benevolence in people that would flourish naturally.

America offered Jefferson fertile soil for seeding such new political plants as free expression, political participation, and limited
government. Like many a political theorist, Jefferson examined his
own heart to find a formula for the ideal government; there he discovered how much he hated the politics of deference. He concluded that his countrymen had to break with the mores of the past
as much as with its monarchical politics. Or, more precisely, he saw
in the typical American assertiveness human material crying out for
political validation. Sometimes superficial, often optimistic without
sufficient warrant, Jefferson established a powerful tie between
ordinary citizens and their government. He gave himself over to
American possibilities and forgot the dreary lessons history taught.
Even in old age, he clung to the sunny side of the street. Writing a
friend in 1817, he floated again his optimistic balloon: "My theory
has always been, that if we are to dream, the flatteries of hope are as
cheap, and pleasanter than the gloom of despair."

3

Interpreting the Constitution
in a Republican Fashion

Jefferson had not been in office seven months before the *Connecticut Courant* called for his impeachment. Summoning a constitutional remedy like impeachment to rid themselves of this interloper seemed appropriate to the Federalists. They had come to think of themselves as the custodians of the Constitution, a sacred text now put in jeopardy by the new president's wildly unorthodox views. Alexander Hamilton, who justly considered himself an expert on the Constitution, led the Federalists from his stronghold in New York politics. A luminary of the Manhattan bar, he also furnished most of the ideas for the party's new voice, the *New York Journal*. Hamilton's admirers did not include Jefferson, who had no doubts about his own reading of the Constitution. Although he had been in Paris during its writing, he was certain that the president should take the lead in interpreting the Constitution. Wresting the new frame of government from the wrongheaded Federalists had been one of his principal motives for going into opposition eight years earlier. Jefferson and Hamilton were ready to take each other on. Rarely has the country witnessed such clashes between two leaders hyperconfident of their understanding of the Constitution. In quick succession, questions about the president's powers, the independence of the judiciary, and the relation of church and state arose to publicize the range of opinions about what the Constitution actually said.

Jefferson's election threw into high relief the unpleasant reality that all constitutions are open to interpretation. With Federalists and Republicans split over political fundamentals, the Constitution became a political football. Its newness exacerbated the situation. It had yet to be determined who had the definitive power to decide constitutional cases. The Constitution itself had not invested that power anywhere. Initially, people looked to the thirty-nine men who had actually signed the document, but the signers failed to form a consensus when a constitutional issue erupted unexpectedly during the very first session of Congress.

Hamilton, then Washington's secretary of the treasury, wanted a quasi-public bank as a capstone to his grand fiscal program. His allies introduced a bill to incorporate such a bank. All was smooth sailing until someone asked whether Congress possessed the authority to establish corporations. The Constitution certainly did not grant such authority explicitly; it would have to be inferred. Hamilton, Washington, Madison, and Attorney General Edmund Randolph— all members of the Constitutional Convention—could not agree on the bill's constitutionality. In a quandry and not wishing to proceed unconstitutionally, Washington turned to his principal cabinet officers for their opinions. In response, Jefferson penned his famous explanation of why the "necessary and proper clause" written into Article One's enumeration of Congress's powers strictly limited Congress's legislative scope.

Hamilton reasoned differently. "Necessary and proper" should be broadly interpreted, he said, as meaning facilitative. No one doubted that a bank would facilitate the borrowing or issuing of money, two powers the Constitution had specifically given Congress. Semantics trumped original intent. In the end, Washington sided with Hamilton, a rebuff that pushed Jefferson closer to open opposition. Now, a decade later, their positions had been reversed. With Washington dead and Adams repudiated at the polls, Hamilton headed the disavowed Federalists, and Jefferson, invested with the authority of the president, moved determinedly to act on his strict constructionist views. It looked as though Jefferson had lost the early battle but had gone on to win the war.

Jefferson's reading of the document—no doubt bolstered by conversations with James Madison—convinced him that the listing of congressional powers in Article One was meant to restrict legislative authority. The Constitution had created a central government, but it had simultaneously limited that government's powers. Jefferson's experience in Virginia politics had heightened his apprehension that lawmakers might run roughshod over constitutions. If legislators chose to ignore constitutional provisions, and the executive and judiciary were supine, constitutions were but paper tigers. And "173 tyrants is not the government we fought for," he wrote then, drawing attention to the potential abusiveness of majority rule that found nothing to restrain it.

Today it's hard to imagine theory playing a critical role in politics, but two hundred years ago, debates about the ends of government excited the interest of most American voters. Adams, when he was vice president, wrote a lengthy tome warning of the historic dangers of men's lust for power. Jefferson rarely composed a letter, address, or report without including a bit of political philosophy, while Hamilton circulated his ideas in newspaper columns sparkling with wit and lucidity. Each saw a bogey threatening the new nation. Chaos scared Hamilton more than the overreaching power of government, which haunted Jefferson. Adams worried about unbalanced government. Unlike the Federalists, Jefferson tolerated dustups and dissent, fearing instead government's tendency to be oppressive. He placed his faith in men's capacity to live peacefully and cooperatively, and he strove to limit formal power that they might have the space to do so. Freedom for him meant throwing off the tutelage of princes, preachers, and patriarchs. Popular with ordinary men, these views continued to distress conservatives, who still hoped that their social inferiors would come to their senses.

Having swallowed their own scare reports, New England Federalists tended to view their electoral defeat more as a national catastrophe than as a personal loss. Their ministers inveighed against Jefferson, the infidel; their political leaders warned that democracy would destroy the republic. Virtuous anxieties cloaked self-interest. Sound governance, to them, meant passing offices from one generation of virtuous men to the next, preferably their sons and nephews. What was to happen to the country when positions of trust passed to men whose only merit was that they had voted for Jefferson?

Abstract worries became concrete issues once Jefferson took office. Two months into his presidency, the Tripolitan crisis provoked Hamilton's first intervention as opposition leader (how strange that label must have seemed to the born-to-rule Federalists!). After the pasha of Tripoli insulted the United States, Jefferson, who never liked paying the bribes extracted by Barbary Coast potentates, refused to negotiate a new treaty. Instead, he sent a naval squadron to the area. An American schooner appropriately named *Enterprise* attacked a Tripolitan polacca. When Congress finally convened, Jefferson asked for retroactive approval, taking the occasion to introduce his view that any military action more than merely defensive required the sanction of Congress. Hamilton pounced on this interpretation of the Constitution immediately. Writing in the *New York Journal*, he stated unequivocally that Congress need not be consulted when a president responded to an attack. He clearly saw in Jefferson's punctiliousness a dangerous diminution of presidential authority. With characteristic hyperbole, Hamilton queried his readers: "What will the world think of the fold which has such a shepherd."[1]

Like Hamilton, Jefferson sought occasions for expounding the meaning of the Constitution. Preparing his first annual message to Congress, he drafted a long disquisition on the unconstitutionality of the Sedition Act. Even though the law had lapsed with the end of Adams's term, he wanted to make public his opinion that the president, no less than Congress and the Supreme Court, had the power to interpret the Constitution. Exercising his "free and independent judgment," he explained, he had compared the Sedition Act with the law of the land and found it "in palpable and unqualified contradiction to the constitution." His cabinet considered this remark gratuitous and persuaded him to remove it, but he did not abandon his conviction that the president is obliged to instruct the nation on constitutional issues.

Sedition was a sensitive touchstone of political sympathies in 1800. The act criminalized political expression by making it an offense to say or publish anything that might bring the government or its officers into disrepute. Great Britain had a draconian sedition law because those gentlemen who composed "the political nation" agreed that the social order was far too fragile to be exposed to the rough-and-tumble of public criticism. Freedom of the press in this most liberal of monarchies meant that there was no prior restraint: anything could be published without advance permission from the crown. But once an item had been published it could be evidence of sedition, just as today a publication can be evidence of slander. Americans had left the British empire, but many of them had not shed colonial sensibilities. Noisy disputes among ordinary citizens about official conduct still offended them. In 1798, the Federalists passed the Sedition Act to rein in what they considered the excesses of democracy.

Illustrative of these attitudes is George Washington's reaction when men—usually men of a Jeffersonian persuasion—formed clubs for the express purpose of talking about politics. Could anything, he asked rhetorically, be more "absurd, more arrogant, or more pernicious to the peace of Society than for self created bodies, forming themselves into permanent Censors, and under the shade of Night in a Conclave" to discuss acts of Congress, which had already "undergone the most deliberate and solemn discussion?" For Jefferson, the answer would have been yes: more absurd was the effort of gentlemen to monopolize politics under the guise of saving people from themselves.[2]

In their attacks, the Federalists proved just as vociferous as the Republicans had been before Jefferson's election. Given the escalating scurrility of partisan journalism, they were probably worse offenders than the Republicans, but Jefferson took pride in tolerating their "falsehoods, calumnies and audacities." He liked to impress foreign visitors with evidence of the country's free press. When Alexander von Humboldt expressed shock at what was said about the president in a newspaper he found at the White House, Jefferson told him to put it in his pocket and, should anyone question America's freedom of speech, "show this paper, and tell where you found it."[3] He believed that speech might be seditious, but he was appalled to see sedition prosecutions used as a tool to crush an opposition.

Republicans in the states took a less relaxed view. The governor of Pennsylvania, Thomas McKean, protested to Jefferson that the Federalist libels were intolerable. And since Jefferson thought that jurisdiction over sedition belonged to the states, he approved of actions taken against Federalist editors in New York and in Pennsylvania, who were tried for seditious libel in 1804 and 1805. Eager to appear consistent, Jefferson offered the rationalization that since the Federalists had switched from repression to licentiousness to destroy the press, a few prosecutions would be in order. "The federalists having failed in destroying the freedom of the press by their gag-law," he wrote McKean, "seem to have attacked it in an opposite form, that is by pushing its licentiousness & its lying to such a degree of prostitution as to deprive it of all credit."

In January 1802, Jefferson had another opportunity to elaborate his take on the Constitution, this time marching into the thorny thicket of state-church relations. The Danbury Baptist Association of Connecticut conveyed to him their delight at his election and requested that he declare a day of fasting to speed the nation's recovery from the acrimony of the recent presidential campaign. With alacrity, Jefferson turned the Baptists down. This was the occasion that he had been waiting for. His response became his most resonant statement about the Constitution, an eighty-three-word sentence that confidently asserted that the first amendment had built "a wall of separation between church and State."[4] Rarely has a metaphor taken on such portentous meaning. At last the second shoe could drop. Twenty-five years earlier, he had drafted the Virginia statute for religious freedom, which the Assembly passed in

1786. Now Jefferson felt that the relation of the federal government to organized religion needed clarification.

In religious matters, the United States was an anomaly; most countries conferred a monopoly of religious authority upon a state church. The American colonies had had two such establishments: the Congregational churches that the Puritans founded throughout New England, and the Church of England, which the mother country had put in place in the southern colonies and the city of New York. Elsewhere in the colonies, official religion was absent and a crazy quilt of Baptists, Moravians, and Quakers flourished alongside unestablished Presbyterian, Lutheran, and Dutch Reformed churches, with a handful of Jewish and Catholic congregations scattered among them.

The American experience of religious pluralism fired reformers with the hope of total freedom from autocratic churches. Jefferson had no sooner returned home from the Second Continental Congress in 1776 than he made plans to eradicate the "spiritual tyranny" of Virginia's Anglican establishment. Scouring Virginia's law books for evidence of abusive power, he uncovered statutes that empowered magistrates to take away the children of freethinking parents and enjoined imprisonment for those who denied the Trinity. With his usual thoroughness, he spent six years herding those laws toward extinction. Virginia's Quakers, Presbyterians, and Baptists joined forces with Jefferson and other rationalists to strip the Church of England—now called the Episcopal Church—of all its privileges and powers, from which they had long suffered. The Bill for Establishing Religious Freedom declared grandly "that no man shall be compelled to frequent or support any religious worship, place, or ministry whatsoever, nor shall be enforced, restrained, molested, or burthened in his body or goods, nor shall otherwise suffer on account of his religious opinions or belief."

Religion continued to fascinate Jefferson, and his religious position intrigued the nation. To the Federalists he was a dangerous atheist whose one book, *Notes on the State of Virginia*, gave proof of his heresies. A much-quoted pamphlet charged Jefferson with rejecting Holy Scripture, in particular the biblical account of the Flood. Citing passages from Jefferson's *Notes*, the Reverend William Linn warned that anyone who avowed such things would destroy religion, introduce immorality, and loosen all the bonds of society. "The voice of the nation in calling a deist to the first office must be construed into no less than a rebellion against God," he intoned. Jefferson's evident talents made him even more of a threat in the eyes of New England's orthodox Calvinists. Yale's president, Timothy Dwight, conjured up a horrifying scene of children "united in chanting mockeries against God," should Republicans be elected. A Federalist newspaper explained that the voters' choice was one between "God and a Religious President" or "Jefferson and no God."[5]

The Danbury Baptists had given Jefferson a chance, as he expressed it, to sow some "useful truths & principles" that "might germinate and become rooted among" the people. He used his own spiritual freedom to seek moral truth, a quest that he shared with his closest friends. Convinced that the Gospels contained spurious verses, he set out to extract the pure and undiluted truths of Jesus from the corrupted dross around them, wielding scissors on two copies of the New Testament.[6] With characteristic confidence, Jefferson claimed that his Gospel contained only the authentic passages about Christ's life and teachings, which stood out like "diamonds in a dunghill." These were not sentiments likely to win the favor of conventional Christians. Nor was the fact that grace was never said at dinner parties, either at the White House or at Monticello. Yet Jefferson regularly attended services, in Washington during his presidency and at the parish church near Monticello when he was home.

Asked by a supporter to spell out his position, Jefferson declared simply, "I am for freedom of religion, and against all maneuvres to bring about a legal ascendancy of one sect over another." Baptists like those in Connecticut approved, even if he had disappointed them in the matter of the day of fasting. The president's position offered the Baptists hope of future protection from the established churches, which still enjoyed tax support along with legal privileges that made it difficult for dissenters to preach or to perform weddings and baptisms. Because the First Amendment dealt only with federal authority, New England's Congregational establishments survived into the nineteenth century. Loath to go with the flow of religious tolerance, Connecticut's legislature passed a law in 1808 making adherence to deism a felony. Only in retrospect does the issue of religious orthodoxy seem exaggerated.

Attitudes toward organized religion were but the most conspicuous of the differences between political contenders in the early Republic. The partisan volleys fired during the campaign of 1800 left battlefields covered with victims. Recriminations punctuated the opening sessions of Jefferson's first Congress. Republicans were still smarting from the vindictiveness with which Federalist judges had prosecuted sedition cases. Nor had their outrage abated over the Judiciary Act of 1801. Passed in the lame-duck days of the Adams presidency, it created a new system of circuit courts designed to move commercial litigation from state to federal courts. It also added sixteen new judgeships to the federal bench, posts that Adams quickly filled with his partisans to establish firm Federalist control of the judiciary.

Certain that there was no demonstrable need for these new judges, Republicans moved to repeal the act, setting off the most acrimonious battle that Congress had yet seen. The Federalists cried foul at the idea of abolishing judgeships already occupied. This would impinge on the independence of the judiciary! A newspaper described the repeal effort as "a wanton, if not a perfidious abuse of power." Crowding onto this high ground, the Federalists harangued their congressional colleagues for weeks. Representative James Bayard spent seven hours in front of a full House and gallery detailing how the Constitution was being traduced by wicked, power-seeking radicals. Never one to quail before an opponent's principles, Virginia's Republican maverick, John Randolph, rejoined by asking whether or not "the creation of new and unnecessary offices, as a provision for political partisans, is an evil more to be dreaded than the abolition of useless ones?"[7]

Since nary a Republican sat on the federal bench, Jefferson

maintained that the Federalists had already politicized the judiciary. "They expect to frighten us," he commented after receiving word
of Bayard's marathon speech, "but are met with perfect sangfroid."
The repeal squeaked by with a one-vote margin after a series of legislative maneuvers that revealed the vice president as a schemer
prepared to court Federalist votes for his own purposes. Intrigue
insinuated itself into profound differences of principle and perception.

Earlier in this season of rancor, William Marbury, one of Adams's
forty-one midnight appointments of justices of the peace, set in
motion litigation that would culminate in a Supreme Court decision with far-reaching impact. Marbury's commission had not actually been delivered before Adams left office; Jefferson ordered
Madison, his secretary of state, to withhold it. Marbury, and several
others who had been denied their appointments as JPs in the new
District of Columbia, sought a writ of mandamus from the U.S.
Supreme Court to force Madison's hand. While writs of mandamus
were ordinary court orders, only courts of original jurisdiction—
courts that conducted the first trial in a case—could issue them.
The Constitution had confined the Supreme Court to appellate
cases, that is, to reviewing the decisions of lower courts. Demonstrating what a virtuoso of legal reasoning he could be, Marshall
turned this small distinction into a major—perhaps the major—
victory for the Supreme Court. As he put it, "the question, whether
an act repugnant to the constitution can become the law of the
land, is a question deeply interesting to the United States; but, happily not of an intricacy proportioned to its interest."

The act possibly "repugnant" to the Constitution was the Judiciary Act of 1789, which had given the Supreme Court the power
to issue writs of mandamus despite the absence of constitutional
authority to do so. The upshot of Marshall's 1803 decision was that
Marbury, though legitimately aggrieved, could not get his commission because the Supreme Court did not have the power to force
Secretary of State Madison to deliver it. While making this case,
Marshall wrote into the law of the land the Supreme Court's

authority to declare congressional acts unconstitutional, a power not found in that same Constitution. Within a week of the repeal of one Judiciary Act, *Marbury v. Madison* rendered unconstitutional parts of an earlier one! Evidently it had been easier for America's leaders to write the Constitution than to be governed by it.

Most of what Americans wanted to do in the early nineteenth century they could do without the help of the federal government. The one great exception was the acquisition of land in the West. Eastern leaders as well as those eager to move onto the frontier wanted to see the country's boundaries move westward. Timothy Dwight caught the spirit of America's continental expansion in his much-loved poem "Greenfield Hill":

> *All hail, thou western world! By heaven design'd*
> *Th' example bright, to renovate mankind.*
> *Soon shall thy sons across the mainland roam*
> *And claim on far Pacific shores, their home . . .*

Dwight wrote this in 1794, while Spain and Great Britain retained possession of the lands abutting the Pacific—and most of the territory between the two oceans as well.

So long as enfeebled Spain nominally controlled the area, Americans were at ease: Spain's dependence upon their trade and migration into the region made it likely that New Orleans and Florida would eventually become part of the United States. Louisiana's Spanish governor, the Baron de Carondelet, indicated as much when he warned his superiors that Americans—"a new and vigorous people"—were "advancing and multiplying in the silence of peace." All this changed in 1801 when Napoleon Bonaparte, the new ruler of France, secured from Spain a retrocession of Louisiana. Even worse for American expectations, the First Consul had grand plans to reestablish a French empire in the New World. Word of these ambitions startled Americans from their daydream of western territories dropping into their laps like so many ripe plums.

American independence and the quickening pace of the Atlantic

trade enhanced the importance of New Orleans. Coveted by
Britain as well as France, Spain, and the United States, this gateway
to the Mississippi Valley became a prime target of European rivalries. People in the United States viewed New Orleans as more a
necessity than a luxury. Federalists felt distress no less extreme than
that of Republicans at the thought of having Napoleon on their
doorstep. The parties differed only in approach, the Federalists
favoring immediate conquest. As one wrote, both Spain and France
must "be driven into the Gulf of Mexico, or we shall never sleep in
peace." Jefferson was no less determined to thwart the rising power
of France, but he preferred an assertive diplomatic campaign to buy
the city, using threats, bullying, and explanations of cold realities,
mixed with occasional pleas, to close the deal. No one asked what
the Constitution had to say about expansion through conquest.

The president dispatched his protégé James Monroe to help
Robert R. Livingston, America's ambassador to France, in the negotiations. As minister plenipotentiary and envoy extraordinary, Monroe was instructed to purchase New Orleans and the Floridas (U.S.
officials were under the mistaken impression that Spain had returned
East and West Florida to France as well).

Developments elsewhere in the Caribbean played into Jefferson's strategy of buying New Orleans. Santo Domingo, where
French troops were struggling to defeat Haitian rebels, turned into
a deathtrap. Renewed hostilities between France and Great Britain
were imminent. Taking all this in and acting with typical impulsive-
ness, Napoleon decided to rid himself of the whole Louisiana Territory in one grand sale. In December 1803, the French governor
officially delivered Louisiana to the United States, thirty-one short
months after Jefferson had received the first credible reports of
Louisiana's return to France in May 1801.[8]

Once the purchase was clinched, some Federalists turned churl-
ish. Hamilton denied that Jefferson's success was due to "any wise
or vigorous measures on the part of the American government," laying success instead at the feet of "a fortuitous concurrence of unforeseen and unexpected circumstances" and "an over-ruling Providence."

Others denied Jefferson political advantage by belittling the purchase; one commentator described Louisiana as a "wilderness unpeopled with any beings except wolves and wandering Indians," which would be "turned into additional states that confirm Virginia's dominance in the union." Another critic exclaimed in mock astonishment: "We are to give money of which we have too little for land of which we already have too much." It *was* a lot of land— 883,000 square miles—and the $15 million purchase price was large enough to necessitate some fancy foreign borrowing. As big as Great Britain, France, Germany, Italy, Spain, and Portugal added together, the Louisiana territory almost doubled America's national domain. An immediate and portentous use was found for the "unpeopled" land when official notice that Indians would be moved west of the Mississippi appeared in the Louisiana Territory Act.

Jefferson, the strict constructionist, has been lambasted for violating his own principles in purchasing Louisiana. Yet if he had, no one seemed to care, for he alone gave serious thought to the constitutional implications of adding such a vast area to the country. During the negotiations, he drafted several versions of an amendment to the Constitution to cover the purchase, but he dropped them when Napoleon insisted on a response within six months. His cabinet members did not share his constitutional scruples—not even Madison, the putative father of the document. The pressure to seize the moment carried the day. The Constitution granted the president the power to negotiate treaties, and American officials regularly acquired land from Indians through treaties. What stretched the president's constitutionally sanctioned treaty-making powers was the incorporation of a foreign population into the union. As it turned out, Jefferson proceeded cautiously in the matter of bringing the people of Louisiana into his "Empire of Liberty," denying them any of the privileges of self-government for a decade. Declaring the Creoles not yet ready for American freedoms, he carried Congress with him. Louisiana did not become a state until 1812.

While Marshall was deliberating Marbury's fate, the Republican-dominated House voted to impeach two Federalist judges, the one

for rank incompetence and the other for spewing partisan vituperation from his bench. Judge John Pickering had clearly gone around
the bend, often presiding over his court while drunk. The Federalists, embarrassed by his conduct, probably would have persuaded
him to resign had they not detested the man Jefferson was likely to
appoint in his place. After a confusing trial, the Senate declared
Pickering guilty of the charges brought by the House. On the same
day—March 12, 1804—House Republicans, flush with success,
gathered enough votes to catch a bigger fish, Supreme Court Justice
Samuel Chase. When looked at together, the two cases suggested
that the Republicans were waging an all-out war on the judiciary—
or at least it did so in the eyes of the Federalists. The wells of bitterness had not yet run dry.

Chase was neither insane nor given to drink. A signer of the Declaration of Independence and a distinguished student of the law, he
had long been a stormy petrel, capable of sending Republicans into
fits of indignation over his high-handed Sedition Act prosecutions.
Observing Chase at the trial of James Callender, a Scottish journalist turned ardent American Republican, Jefferson's son-in-law
described Chase as "indecent and tyrannical." A blustering bully who
used his height, girth, and quick wit to intimidate witnesses and
lawyers alike, Chase excoriated democracy from his bench. With
unmistakable reference to the document he had once proudly signed,
he ridiculed the idea that all men "are entitled to enjoy equal liberty
and equality rights." He predicted that American politics would
"sink into mobocracy—the worst of all possible governments."[9]

To bring Chase down would have assuaged the pain of many, but
it was not to be. The trial fulfilled every expectation of melodrama,
with packed galleries, special boxes for VIPs, and crimson-covered
benches for the twenty-five Republican and nine Federalist senators
arrayed on either side of Vice President Burr as he presided at this
spectacular trial. Eight articles of impeachment were approved by
an overwhelmingly partisan vote, which gave substance to the Federalists' characterization of the impeachment as an assault on judicial independence. Chase's conviction, they predicted, would render

federal courts servile tools of the president and Congress. Enough Republicans agreed; none of the articles of impeachment could muster a two-thirds vote, so the proceedings left Chase an acquitted martyr and, as of 2002, still the only Supreme Court justice ever to be impeached.

The impeachment cases pushed two substantive issues to the fore. The first one had to do with removing unfit judges who held their offices "during good Behavior." The Federalists argued that criminality had to be proven while Republicans tried to use impeachment to get rid of incompetents. After the Pickering trial, Jefferson saw clearly that impeachment was a clumsy tool, but better than nothing. Facing the problem squarely, some Republicans talked of amending the Constitution to provide for the removal of a judge by the president upon the request of Congress. A different view of the judiciary was taken by Republicans grouped around the Philadelphia journalist William Duane. They challenged the very idea of an independent judiciary, which for them held none of the charms that Federalists found in it. They interpreted *independent* to signify the invulnerability of an elite judiciary capable of thwarting laws passed by democratic legislatures.

Chief Justice John Marshall published the first installment of his five-volume *Life of Washington* in 1804. Like Parson Weems, he chose to present the nation's revolutionary hero as a man of rectitude, even at the risk of making him boring. Jefferson bought each volume as it appeared, having them all bound in leather in a handsome matched set. The biography's length did not deter him from viewing it as a partisan pamphlet masquerading as a patriotic tome. Although he remained quiet about it at the time, Jefferson still bristled years later at Marshall's interpretation of the origins of his republican opposition. Marshall, like most Federalists—perhaps this is a litmus test for Federalism—proved incapable of responding to the reformist hope of changing the lot of mankind. Instead, he saw Jefferson as an inordinately ambitious man, truckling to the democratic values of ordinary men to gain popularity and not because he genuinely shared them.

When they spoke of Republicans as men without any fixed principles or as disgruntled visionaries, the Federalists advertised the limits of their own political imagination. They simply could not picture a world run on any other principles than the ones that they had imbibed as schoolboys. They looked to the clergy to articulate national values, and to themselves—members of venerable officeholding families—to guarantee that public authority supported those values. Jefferson was truly a visionary, a man with a vision of a different system. Hostile to the Federalists' state-building, he idealized the informal interactions of free men, sharing Thomas Paine's view, expressed in the opening of *Common Sense*, that society "promotes our happiness positively by uniting our affections" while government only restrains "our vices." As Jefferson wrote a supporter after his first year in office, "The path we have to pursue is so quiet that we have nothing scarcely to propose to our Legislature." "A noiseless course, not meddling with the affairs of others, unattractive of notice, is a mark that the society is going on in happiness," he confidently continued, ending his little homily with the conviction that "if we can prevent the government from wasting the labor of the people, under the pretense of taking care of them, they must become happy."

Once independence had been secured, the men who became Federalists had been ready to settle down and enjoy self-government on pretty much the same social terms that existed in their colonial youth. The boisterous politics that had erupted in many of the states during the fighting of the revolutionary war had convinced them of the need for a stronger hand on the helm. Many of those drawn to the Constitution's creation of a central government hoped that the country might grow more like Great Britain, with its stability, deference, and refinement. They wanted to seal off the revolutionary era and teach a new generation of young Americans the truths of how to secure order. Alexander Hamilton's reaction to Adam Smith's idea of self-regulating economic life is illustrative. He considered commerce without "a common directing power" to be "one of those wild speculative paradoxes, which have grown into credit among us, contrary to the uniform practice and sense of the most enlightened nations."[10] Although he recognized the close connection between economic and political development, he could not conceive of a system with its own dynamic of growth and informal regulation. How deeply disturbing it must have been for the Federalists to have secured the ratification of the Constitution with its promise of an energetic central government and then be forced to contend with ferocious and successful critics of their goals sprung from their own elite ranks!

Looking back we can see that these controversies sculpted American government, giving life to the inert words of the Constitution. Blessed with a brilliant Supreme Court chief justice, the Federalists continued to exercise power through the federal courts while Jefferson put his impress on the executive and legislative branches. If Marshall's lodestar was unquestioned federal authority, Jefferson's was limiting the scope of that authority. To achieve both goals required discipline and persistence, qualities each man possessed to a rare degree. And their work prevailed over decades. Jefferson's influence continued through his successors Madison and Monroe, who shared his admiration for a small, frugal federal government. Marshall sat on the Supreme Court until death ended his tenure in 1835. One might credit the two men with sketching the two faces of American liberalism: minimalist federal rule in deference to the realm of personal freedom and local initiative, and the supremacy of the rule of law protecting that Jeffersonian realm of private, voluntary activities.

Although Jefferson and Marshall disliked each other intensely, their disparate interpretations of the Constitution actually complemented each other, for both strengthened the realm of free association and free bargaining. Looking back at Jefferson with an awareness of the civil war that almost rent the nation asunder, historians have exaggerated his commitment to states' rights. The backward glance at Marshall's career has similarly been affected by knowledge of the importance of corporations and big government in the aftermath of American industrialization. If the sense of what happened after both men died could be erased, we might stress instead Jefferson's national vision of independent farm families planting liberal institutions across the continent. Marshall's assertion of federal over state authority would still be credited, to be sure, but so too would be his protection of the rights of association and free enterprise from unwarranted government intrusion.

Jefferson also explicitly detached liberty from its Spartan connection to self-denial and reattached it to the promise of prosperity. His optimism floated on expectations of material abundance. The goals he articulated when he became president required the expanding frontier of uncultivated land that lay west of the Appalachian Mountains. Too much land, Jefferson believed, fostered the savage condition; but without land, men could not achieve personal autonomy. His draft constitution for Virginia, written in 1776, included a fifty-acre property qualification for voting while simultaneously proposing a gift of fifty acres to all landless adult white men. He even found political significance in the crops grown on American farms. The cultivation of wheat was the exact reverse of labor-intensive tobacco, he wrote in the *Notes*: "Besides cloathing the earth with herbage, and preserving its fertility, it feeds the labourers plentifully, requires from them only moderate toil . . . and diffuses plenty and happiness among the whole."

Spurning Malthus's gloomy prediction that population growth would always outpace food supplies, he insisted that in America, harvests grew exponentially. The opportunity for productive efforts enabled him to square the circle of self-interest and community welfare. "So invariably do the laws of nature create our duties and interests," he wrote the French economist J. B. Say, "that when they seem to be at variance, we ought to suspect some fallacy in our reasoning."[11] One cannot imagine either Hamilton or Marshall subscribing to such a naïve concept of human nature and civic responsibility. Nor have they been given sufficient credit for stabilizing the economic system through which Jefferson's farmers found their happiness.

An uncritical reader of the philosophers of the Enlightenment and an ardent advocate of Baconian science, Jefferson valued theory over experience when that experience tilted its benefits so heavily toward elite privilege. In this, he spoke to the aspirations of ordinary Americans in that critical half-century after independence when a national identity was being formed. He also delivered on his campaign promises, reducing the national debt from $83 million to $77 million and lowering federal spending by 30 percent while virtually eliminating federal taxes and initiating economies that yielded an annual surplus of $2 million. With such success it was easy for him to extol the new world aborning.

Both materialistic and intellectual in his goals, Jefferson envisioned American liberties as facilitators of prosperity. The acquisition of Louisiana promised a protracted mingling of freedom and opportunity. Jefferson said that it would take one hundred generations to reach the Pacific, a prediction Americans trashed by getting there in just three. Preferring always to take the rosiest view of the future, he appealed to optimists, as the Federalists did to pessimists. Jefferson believed that political participation bolstered by basic education would unleash the creative powers of ordinary men. Invention, science, and building projects of all sorts would flourish. His own love of philosophical theories and religious explorations elevated his hopes for what human beings would accomplish if given scope for action. Adams commented years later that Jefferson's taste was "judicious in liking better the dreams of the Future, than the History of the Past."[12] If Jefferson had chosen not to run for a second term, he could have kept intact those dreams of the future that his initial successes did so much to bolster.

4

A Painful Reelection

The presidential election dominated politics throughout 1804. A Republican caucus in Congress renominated Jefferson without dissent in February while it just as emphatically dropped Vice President Burr from the ticket. During the course of the year, enough states ratified the Twelfth Amendment, separating the Electoral College ballots for president and vice president, to put it into effect for this election. The campaign itself turned nasty, and a dramatic duel between two old political enemies captured the public's attention during the summer. The Federalists, who were genuine opponents of slavery, tried to awaken voters with a scandalous charge against the president, but the electorate remained fixed on the Republican formulation of the contest: advance toward full democracy, or retreat to the elitism of Eastern reactionaries.

Jefferson's heart lay elsewhere that year: his twenty-five-year-old daughter Maria Jefferson Eppes died on April 17, thirteen days after he returned from Washington to Monticello. Polly, as Maria was called, was the fifth child Jefferson had buried, though the others had died in infancy. Now there was only his eldest daughter, Martha, with her many children, to leaven the burden of his public responsibilities. In a letter to a friend, Jefferson's grief merged with self-pity: "[M]y evening prospects now hang on the slender thread of a single life."

Abigail Adams had helped Polly years earlier, when as a nine-year-old she landed in London accompanied by her maid, Sally Hemings. Polly stayed with the Adamses for several weeks before traveling on to Paris to join her father, who was then serving as minister to France. Memories of that pleasant interlude momentarily dissolved the bitterness that had soured the friendship between Jefferson and the Adamses. In her letter to the president, Abigail Adams wrote that a newspaper account of Polly's death had "burst through" her restraint. In his reply, Jefferson warmly reassured her of an esteem that had "never been lessened for a single moment." Warily the two old friends went over the grounds for their mutual disappointments and suspicions. Though they exchanged five more letters, they failed to move beyond a frank canvassing of the animosities that had driven them apart.

Adams was particularly unhappy because Jefferson had freed James Callender. A Scotsman who had fled Britain in 1793 to escape prosecution for a pamphlet espousing Scottish nationalism, Callender got caught up in the Jeffersonian movement once he arrived in the United States. He had a caustic pen that deeply rankled those he pilloried. Adams took very personally Callender's unkind characterization of her husband—"the basest Libel, the lowest and vilest Slander which malice could invent," she called it. Callender had already besmirched the reputation of Alexander Hamilton when he publicized Hamilton's involvement with Maria Reynolds and her blackmailing husband. It was said that Callender's attacks inspired the Sedition Act of 1798, under which he was imprisoned in the waning days of Adams's presidency.

While Jefferson confessed to Adams that he had come to disapprove of Callender's coarse and scurrilous writings, he disliked the Federalists' wholesale attack on Republican polemics even more. He recognized the legitimacy of some sedition prosecutions, but, as he interpreted events, the Federalists had used the pretext of protecting reputations to poison the lifeblood of republics: the free circulation of opinion. Where Adams saw personal insult, Jefferson affirmed political principle. There was no meeting of minds or hearts, but these former friends did leave posterity a fascinating recapitulation of the issues that then inflamed American politics.

Callender died in 1803—fittingly, his enemies would have said, by plunging into the James River while drunk. Before his death he roiled the political waters one last time when he turned against his benefactor. Jefferson had released him from jail—even remitted his fine—but Callender felt that as a martyr to civil liberties he deserved more, specifically an appointment as Richmond's postmaster. The president turned him down. Never a man to take a rebuff with equanimity, Callender began sniping at the Republicans in his newspaper, the *Richmond Recorder*. Then, in September 1802, he dropped a bombshell, audaciously asserting that Jefferson kept an "African venus" as his concubine. He identified the woman as Sally Hemings, the slave who had accompanied Polly Jefferson to France in 1787. Federalists reveled in this rumor, filling their newspapers with satires, skits, and doggerel about Jefferson's "sable beauty," conjuring up a "Congo" harem in Monticello. Even proper young John Quincy Adams stooped to publishing—in the *Port Folio*, the Federalists' principal journal—an anonymous ode alluding to Jefferson's illicit liaison.[1]

The Hemings affair has dogged Jefferson's reputation ever since, believed and disbelieved in by turns for two centuries. In its strongest form, the charge is that Jefferson and Sally Hemings began a liaison when they were in Paris together. Abigail Adams's depiction of Hemings as "quite a child" doesn't support this version, nor is there strong proof that Hemings had a baby then. Jefferson's Farm Book lists five births for her, the first in 1795 when she was twenty-two; her last child, Eston Hemings, arrived in 1808. Scholars have wrestled with fragments of evidence for years, trying to work out whether they were dealing with suppressed facts or slander. Some took umbrage at the affront to Jefferson's rectitude; others suggested that the white father of Sally Hemings's children was more likely one of Jefferson's nephews, a possibility that has since been disproved. The record is silent about the form the Hemings-

Jefferson relationship might have taken, leaving commentators a clean canvas upon which to paint a loving intimacy or a cruel exercise of white male power.

In 1998, DNA testing established that a Jefferson male had fathered Eston Hemings. Given such stunning confirmation of Callender's charge, historians are now inclined to believe that Jefferson fathered all of Sally Hemings's children. This hypothesis is supported by the fact that in his Farm Book Jefferson did not name the father of Sally Hemings's children; the Farm Book entries for other slave births do include the father's name. Possibly, Eston Hemings was the sole child that Sally Hemings and Jefferson had together. If so, Jefferson did not lie when, during the 1804 campaign, he addressed the rumor obliquely. He wrote to several of his cabinet members, acknowledging the accuracy of a different item of gossip about him. It was, he said, the only bit of Federalist calumny that was true—a statement that could be construed as a denial of the Hemings affair, the principal subject of Federalist vilification that season. In 1873, almost half a century after Jefferson's death, an Ohio newspaper published the autobiography of Sally Hemings's son Madison. Madison Hemings claimed that his mother had identified Jefferson as the father of her children.

A dissenting group of scholars has challenged the idea that the DNA findings established Jefferson as the father of Eston Hemings.[2] Because Jefferson had no male heir, and DNA can establish paternity only through an unbroken male line, researchers testing the linkage used tissue taken from a living descendant of Jefferson's brother. Critics of the DNA study point to the fact that there were eighteen Jefferson men in Virginia during the period when Hemings had her children who could have been the father, though only Jefferson lived in close proximity to her.

But even if he was not involved with Hemings, Jefferson did not escape connection with the tortured sexual liaisons that slavery fostered. He acquired the Hemings family from his father-in-law, who was widely believed to have had a long-term relationship with Betty Hemings. This would make Sally Hemings, Betty's daughter, the half sister of Martha Wayles Jefferson, Jefferson's beloved wife. Members of the Hemings family—Sally's sisters and brothers and her own children—were the only slaves Jefferson freed at his death. He also petitioned the legislature to let them continue to live in Virginia, as an exception to the law that stipulated that all manu-mitted slaves had to leave the state within a year. While coerced sexual relations with slaves were common throughout the South, Jefferson's liaison is particularly troubling: it was he whose words tied American independence to a ringing endorsement of natural rights. Yet Jefferson also held the unshakable conviction that the white and black races could not and should not live together in freedom.

An opponent of slavery—at least in his rhetoric—Jefferson maintained throughout his life that the very experience of being either a slave or a slave master made it impossible to live in a free, biracial society. In his *Notes* he spelled out why:

> Deep rooted prejudices entertained by the whites; ten thousand recollections, by the blacks, of the injuries they have sustained; new provocations; the real distinction which nature has made; and many other circumstances, will . . . pro-duce convulsions which will probably never end but in the extermination of the one or the other race.

Such a bleak view of the incompatibility of Africans and Europeans leaves a child of mixed heritage doubly damned. It also starkly clari-fies Jefferson's conception of an "Empire of Liberty" as being for whites only.

There is no doubt that Jefferson considered Negroes inferior to whites. He said so in his one book, *Notes on the State of Virginia*, but he also blamed slavery for the degradation of the enslaved and explicitly affirmed that human liberty was based on natural rights, not on intelligence. Nor did his suspicions about the inferiority of African Americans prevent his appointing the black astronomer and mathematician Benjamin Banneker to the post of official sur-veyor for the District of Columbia.

In the abstract, slavery scratched at his conscience, but in practice, Jefferson accepted the institution pretty much as he found it, going along with the norms of his fellow planters. He treated his slaves as possessions, offering their labor to his sons-in-law as gestures of generosity. He personally got rid of slaves whom he considered insubordinate, and he sold slaves when he was short of money. Serving on the committee to revise Virginia's laws after Independence, Jefferson wrote severe physical punishments into the state's new slave code. Only when he discussed slavery as an institution did his rhetoric soar. Otherwise he could be quite matter-of-fact, as when he explained to an English correspondent who was contemplating a move to Virginia that "white laborers may be hired, but they are less subordinate, their wages higher, and their nourishment much more expensive." Or crassly calculating, as when he commented on the superior value of female slaves: "I consider a woman who brings a child every two years as more profitable than the best man of the farm. What she produces is an addition to the capital, while his labor disappears in mere consumption."

Jefferson could have disentangled himself from the South's peculiar institution. Thousands of slave owners did, many of them touched by the brief antislavery crusade of the Methodists and Baptists. One particularly eloquent Baptist preacher traveled with manumission forms in his saddlebags. In 1782, Virginia legislators had even made it easier to free human property, the statute requiring freed slaves to leave the state within a year not being passed until 1806. Jefferson was also a witness to Northern emancipation, as one by one the states above the Mason-Dixon Line put slavery on the path to legal extinction. These acts brought the issue out of the study and into the political realm, demonstrating that legislation could end the most ancient and odious of all labor systems. A world without slavery was imaginable; realizing such an end was on the agenda of dozens of conscientious people, but not on Jefferson's.

Jefferson's excuse was that slavery had been entailed upon his generation; while true, this hardly explains why a man of such progressive ideals failed to keep up with those who were devising ways to rid the country of the worst offense against human freedom and dignity. He could never subdue the turmoil the subject aroused in him, and his opinions changed over the course of his long career. The high point of his efforts against slavery came when, as a member of the Continental Congress, he proposed banishing slavery in the territories beyond the Appalachian Mountains, north and south, by 1800. His plan failed by a single vote, but clearly inspired the ban on slavery's westward spread that appeared in the Northwest Ordinance of 1787.

Nowhere is Jefferson's selective embrace of natural rights more starkly revealed than in his presidential treatment of the Haitian rebels. Beginning in 1791, enslaved and free blacks on the French half of the Caribbean sugar island of Hispaniola fought furiously to expel the French, not unlike the Americans fighting the British a generation earlier. Under the inspired leadership of François-Dominique Toussaint-Louverture, they made themselves and their country—renamed Haiti—free. Washington recognized the authority of General Toussaint-Louverture, but France and England in turn sought to overthrow the "Bonaparte of the Antilles." Napoleon's plans for reestablishing France's North American empire hinged on reasserting control of Saint-Domingue. Through a horrendous decade of disease, warfare, and civil strife, the Haitians prevailed. Coming into the presidency, Jefferson withheld diplomatic recognition from them. When Toussaint-Louverture discovered that Jefferson's emissary did not have diplomatic standing, he took it as an insult and stormed from the room.

Jefferson tacked back and forth in his Haitian course, tolerating American trade with Haiti when it looked as if the rebels might prevent Napoleon from reestablishing a French empire in the New World, and at the same time hinting to Napoleon's ministers that he would not block French repossession of Saint-Domingue if Louisiana were left with Spain. What Jefferson clearly never did was hail the Haitian Revolution as the first successful slave revolt and Haiti as the Western Hemisphere's second republic. Faced with blacks demonstrating a taste and talent for freedom, he recoiled like any other slave owner. He saw Haiti more as a threat to Southern slavery than as a beacon of freedom.

When the Haitian rebellion was followed by a narrowly averted slave uprising, the Gabriel Prosser revolt, in Virginia in 1800, Southern equivocation on slavery ended: slavery should be considered permanent in the United States, the rights of slave owners honored like those of any other property owner. For American Southerners, Haiti remained a troubling presence, a sign of the violent potential of slavery and a reminder of the resistance that their own slaves had shown during the American Revolution. Haitian French slave owners fleeing to the United States brought horror stories of pillage and bloodshed, stories that Southerners retold whenever pertinent. In 1804, New Jersey became the last Northern state to set a date for ending slavery within its borders, but despite the existence of a bloc of free states, the singleness of purpose among Southern leaders prevailed when the issue of slavery came before Congress. Slave revolts confirmed the odiousness of the institution, but frightened as they educated. How apt Jefferson's depiction of slave owners as having the wolf by the tail!

The successful slave rebellion in Haiti and the aborted slave revolt in Richmond shocked Southern slaveholders out of their complacency. Frightened Virginia officials executed twenty-five slaves after the Prosser plan was discovered. Trying to restore calm, Jefferson—who favored deportations over executions—wrote James Monroe, then Virginia's governor, that there "is strong sentiment that there has been hanging enough," adding "the other states and the world as large will forever condemn us if we indulge in a principle of revenge, or go one step beyond absolute necessity." Of course it was in the nature of the institution of slavery to generate such awful necessities.

In the political climate of the election year, 1804, rumors of sexual promiscuity and religious infidelity could not diminish the president's popularity. Throughout his first term, Jefferson had impressed his values upon his party and deftly managed to keep in good standing with both radical and moderate Republicans. Quite the opposite of Burr, for whom the party's interests took a distant second place to his own. Burr's angling for the presidency after the 1800 tie vote sealed his fate with congressional Republicans, most of whom found his subsequent political dealings duplicitous at best.

After a canvass of several favorite sons, the Republicans chose sixty-five-year-old George Clinton for the vice presidential slot. A brigadier general in the Continental Army, Clinton had led the common farmers of New York in their political struggles against that state's entrenched aristocratic families and had naturally gravitated to the Jeffersonian movement in the 1790s, when he was serving as governor. Unlike the Republicans, the Federalists were reluctant to nominate anyone for president or vice president, leaving the choice to whatever Federalists were chosen as electors. Privately, they decided on Charles Cotesworth Pinckney of South Carolina and Rufus King of New York as their presidential and vice presidential candidates. In the end, Federalists fielded slates of electors only in Massachusetts, New Hampshire, and Maryland. It took a long time for them to accept the hurly-burly of party politics.

In making Jefferson's alleged black mistress the centerpiece of their attack, the Federalists were not merely scandalmongering. They were calling the electorate's attention to the contradiction between talking natural rights and enslaving human beings. The Federalists' open hostility to democratic politics and their genuine dislike of slavery played into their acceptance of class differences. Because they believed in social distinctions, they tended to slot black and white laborers together, recognizing the civil rights of both and the political rights of neither. Federalists also blended an Old World recognition of status with an American appreciation of earned merit. Both Washington and Hamilton, their heroes, were self-made men, but men whose ambition it had been to join the upper class, not challenge it. Federalists did not think that ordinary men had much to contribute to public life. So strongly did they hold this conviction that they construed Jefferson's enthusiasm for an expanded realm of popular politics as sheer hypocrisy. What they saw—all they could see—was a man who should have known better pandering to those who knew nothing at all worth knowing.

While rarely considered a notable campaign, that of 1804 reveals just how much events during the thirty years after independence had unsettled Americans. And of course it is during dramatic transformations that people are likely to eliminate the middle ground and divide into radical and conservative camps. Most spectacularly for the underpinnings of American politics, the deference ordinary white men had paid to their social superiors collapsed like a soufflé in the 1780s and 1790s. The Federalists experienced this change as a blow not just to their self-esteem but to their country: they were certain that the nation could never stabilize itself without deference to its leaders and restraint from its citizens. The Massachusetts senator Fisher Ames reflected this view when he warned that "the natural vanity, presumption, and restlessness of the human heart" had always provided safe havens for troublemaking radicals. Where Republicans viewed participatory politics as good for America's future, Federalists saw the politicization of ordinary white men as inimical to self-government and to the virtue and dignity needed to keep in check the rambunctious passions of the mob. The one group celebrated change as democratic progress; the other mourned the destruction of a precious way of governing.

Property and family figured prominently in the Federalists' calibration of political worth. Neither found a place in a democracy—indeed, the Federalists held the term in such contempt that they tried to add it to the Republican party's designation, hoping thereby to stigmatize the Jeffersonians. If the Jeffersonians could be labeled Democratic Republicans instead of just Republicans, Federalists could recover the glorious name *republican* for themselves. According to the *Port Folio*, the Federalists aimed "to present democracy in its native deformity." By stripping off its assumed masks, they could rescue republicanism from the disgrace of "its forced and unnatural association with democracy." The term *republican* could then once again reflect a commitment to a refined liberty achieved through a moral authority based on social cohesion.[3]

Some New England Federalists actually contemplated secession from the Union. Timothy Dwight of Yale expected the American experiment to fail: free governments would survive "only if revealed religion were allowed to create virtuous citizens who would elect virtuous rulers who in their turn would support institutions that created virtue." Theodore Sedgwick, the last Federalist Speaker of the House, lamented that "the aristocracy of virtue is destroyed; personal influence is at an end." More philosophically, Senator Ames advised his fellow Federalists to entrench themselves in state governments and make them "a shelter of the wise, and good, and rich." "I would never have abandoned the government personally," New York's Rufus King announced, "but from the most complete conviction that the people would make an experiment of democracy." This was a bit of bombast, for King ran as the last Federalist candidate for president in 1816, having returned to the Senate earlier.

Federalists' convictions of their own probity and Jeffersonian chicanery were sustained by their analysis of the 1800 presidential election. Here slavery returned to haunt democracy, and the Constitution provided the spell that raised it. One of its three compromises over slavery framed this particular theme of the Federalist campaign. The Founding Fathers agreed in Article 1, section 2 to use three-fifths of the slave population in all calculations of population for the purposes of both taxation and representation. Northerners had wanted to count enslaved men and women at 100 percent for taxation and at nothing for representation. Southerners argued for the opposite: 100 percent for representation and nothing for taxation. Hence the compromise at three-fifths for both. (The entire white population counted for representation, even though children and women couldn't vote.) The compromise over counting slaves mediated the disparate interests of the North and South. More portentously, it gave constitutional legitimacy to slavery by counting human beings as taxable property.

The Federalists calculated that Adams, not Jefferson, would have won the 1800 election had slaves not counted in setting the states' allotment of electors. "None but the stupidest of the rabble [can] be deceived by their hypocrisy, when they dare to say, the will of the people ought to prevail," Ames insisted, adding, "They know that without the black votes, Mr. Jefferson would not have been president; they know that these black votes are given in contempt of the rights of man; for the Virginia negroes have no more political will or power than the cattle on the Kennebec."[4]

Alas for Ames, in 1804 it was a white man's democracy that was struggling to be born. Try as the Federalists might to arouse the electorate to the mischief of using slaves to augment the political representation of slaveholders, the cause of the moment was eliminating ancient privileges of class and status among white males. It was vain to attempt to persuade newly enfranchised men that they should confine themselves to voting and leave the governing to their betters. The new access to politics that Jefferson championed thrilled those weary of the contempt shown them by their social superiors. While many might have opposed slavery, they viewed Federalists' concerns for the black man as casuistic at best. How could they be taken seriously when Federalists openly espoused elite rule and ridiculed the idea of unlearned men talking about public policy?

Despite state property qualifications, a wider array of people could vote in the United States than had ever done so in any country. Their numbers included free blacks in a scattering of states and a handful of single women in New Jersey. Victory at the national level in 1800 encouraged Jeffersonians to agitate at the state level for extensions of the suffrage. Maryland led the way in 1801, with a law abolishing property qualifications and requiring the secret ballot, even though a state constitutional amendment in 1810 withdrew the law's generous provisions from free blacks. Strict residency requirements continued, but the ambit of white citizenship widened; black suffrage grew more slowly, through the enlargement of the free black population. While Virginia, Louisiana, Connecticut, and

Rhode Island retained some form of property qualification until well into the 1840s, most states eliminated it. Propertied women who had voted in New Jersey lost that right in 1807, but entirely new groups of men, including adult sons living at home, apprentices, and wage earners, joined the ranks of citizens. Education was going to erase the differences between different ranks. As one Jeffersonian enthusiast put it, "knowledge is the standing army of Republics."

The discretion that Federalists had practiced when political discussions were confined to small upper-class circles buckled under the onslaught of boisterous public debates. Identified opinions and published disputes cracked open the closed circle of leaders. Enfranchising the propertyless made common men aware of themselves as political participants; even the young demanded their rights. When Harvard authorities ruled in 1798 that no party politics were to be introduced into the public literary exercises at commencement, the undergraduates denounced the decision as an infringement of their right to free speech and refused to give any addresses until a compromise was worked out.

The crucial differences between the Republicans and Federalists played themselves out on the economic field as well. The advantages for ordinary free men of Jefferson's economic policy became apparent during his first term. In many ways it was policymaking by default, its principles being decentralization, noninterference, and the opening of resources to ordinary white men. Hamilton relied on the distance between respectable creditors and poor debtors to make the favored few a powerful prop for the government. Where Federalists had expected the mercantile elite to fund new initiatives with their capital, Jeffersonian policies helped local entrepreneurs build up sweat equity with money borrowed from friends. His emphasis on agricultural prosperity led directly to support of commerce. "It is material to the safety of Republicanism to detach the mercantile interest from its enemies and incorporate them into the body of its friends," he wrote, adding: "A merchant is naturally a

Republican, and can be otherwise only from a vitiated state of things."[5]

Many Jeffersonians looked skeptically on national corporations; in the states, they freely voted charters to new ventures. The proliferation of corporations actually aided ordinary people by creating a transportation infrastructure for farmers, tradesmen, peddlers, and artisans to get to market. It also gave men of modest means access to investments. Far from being a rich man's preserve, banking offered hundreds of local savers an investment possibility. Stalwarts of the old order decried the leveling tendency in easy money policies, but ordinary people resoundingly approved and pressured their states to incorporate road- and canal-building and insurance companies. The three banks in the United States in 1790 were joined by twenty-five new ones in 1800, twenty of them outside the major cities. By 1810, there were 327. During buoyant periods when banknotes gave market participants the wherewithal to carry out their plans, the extra notes were a kind of borrowing against the future, the deployment of faith in lieu of savings.

With once regulated activities now open to all comers, the economy could be construed as voluntary, free, even natural. There was an interesting corollary to this. Hamilton had erected a set of public institutions to keep watch over the economy. Jefferson's election excluded that possibility without uprooting the legal infrastructure for a national market. The less that was heard from conservative politicians about stability, order, and continuity, the less conspicuous became the law's role in facilitating economic initiative. The federal government continued to sell land at administered prices. States conferred licenses, franchises, and bounties on speculative development, but in both cases public authority appeared merely as the handmaiden of private enterprise.

Had the Federalists stayed in office, the course of economic development in the United States would have been guided by government officials attentive to the interests of creditors. The intertwined social and economic perceptions of a national elite would have informed policies for the country as a whole, with a national bank restricting the issue of banknotes. But instead a new political movement explicitly hostile to government authority came to power. Paradoxically, the fiscal stability achieved in Washington's administration redounded to the benefit of ordinary men intent upon liberating themselves from hierarchical institutions. In his Supreme Court decisions, Jefferson's longtime foe John Marshall actually strengthened this tendency to think and act as though economic transactions were a part of a natural, voluntary realm, protected from legislative intrusion. With decisions rendering contracts immune from tampering by state legislatures, Marshall developed a liberal jurisprudence that complemented Jefferson's executive initiatives. By strengthening the constitutional protection of contracts and property, the Supreme Court reduced the scope of federal and state intrusion into American economic life. Reasoning from utility was pushed aside for the rhetoric of sacred rights and inviolable principles (from Marshall) and natural rights (from Jefferson).

Basic to a capitalist economy, of course, is the capital that sets men and women to work making marketable commodities. The United States was not only a debtor nation; it was also a nation of debtors. A web of intricate credit transactions connected virtually all participants in the economy. The rate of growth in the early republic was set in large part by the behavior of ordinary men and women whose propensity to move, to innovate, to accept paper money, to switch quickly from homemade goods once commercial goods were available, hastened the expansion of farming, commerce, credit, and information.

The great beneficiaries of change in the Jeffersonian era were America's white men, regardless of class or rank. They could participate in politics and freely choose their religion (or choose no religion); the common law gave them command over their wives, children, servants, and slaves. Free young men—even some young women—struck out on their own to the West, toward urban opportunity, into new occupations. American geographic mobility astounded foreign visitors who described for friends back home the forests of masts in American harbors and the unending train of wagons snaking their way to Pittsburgh or Cooperstown or Lexington. To them, American society offered an ever-changing visual landscape as people moved, roads were graded, land cleared, and buildings raised in a constant reconfiguration of the material environment. The opening up of public land for private purchase rapidly increased the number of property owners. While many of them became dirt-poor farmers, they had managed to get on the right side of the critical divide between independence and dependency, probably the most salient of all social markers in an America that was still 80 percent rural. People not only moved out; they sometimes moved up, too. This very mobility eroded status markers and scrambled the social codes inherited from a colonial world dominated by aristocratic European values.

Although the revolutionary zeal for change stopped at the threshold of the "castle" in which the "master" reigned supreme over his household, its transforming potential could be seen in everything from the institution of slavery to the conduct of youth. Few American women emerged to urge changes in laws affecting property, divorce, or child custody, yet the generation coming of age after the Revolution grappled with the question of women's status because their lives had begun with a severe rupture in established understandings. It was difficult to keep talk of freedom from spilling out of the formal channels of law and spreading to informal and private areas. Little was done to change the legal restrictions on women's control over their lives, but the outpouring of writings, mostly from men, forced fresh thinking about women's need for schooling and their innate capacities.

Unlike earlier political divisions, the partisanship that had begun in the 1790s changed the relations of voters and officeholders. Vitriolic exchanges engaged the public in disputes that once would have been viewed as beyond their ken. Aggressive newspaper editors discovered and printed the secrets of official business, opening the arcana of government to outside inspection. The anonymous or pseudonymous author gave way to one who signed his pieces. In the course of the long Jeffersonian attack on elite governance, the idea of secrecy lost its supporting rationale that only public figures and their gentlemanly friends could be trusted with important information. Increasingly state business became a kind of public property.

Had the Federalist elite secured its ascendancy, a public realm might have emerged that was bounded by the gentry's sense of discretion. Instead, the effects of expanded publicity became cumulative: a larger pool of readers and a dramatic augmentation in the kinds of conflicts deemed publicizable. Few institutions could protect themselves from public curiosity—not the U.S. Army, the medical profession, or the bishops of the Episcopal Church. Individual Republicans might have acknowledged the evils of the prevailing political mores—certainly Jefferson shrank from the vulgar assaults on officials' reputations—but they all recognized that even unseemly brouhahas over laws and policies were integral to self-government.

Popular dislike of the Federalists' conservative stance tended to neutralize attacks on Jefferson's irreligion. Though Federalist clergy fulminated at the president's heterodoxy, what they really objected to was his opposition to church *establishments*. The Virginia Statute for Religious Freedom of 1786, which ended the Episcopal Church's privileges in that state, had attracted national attention and made Jefferson a hero with the Methodists and Baptists. Flourishing after the Revolution, these two upstart sects had suffered at the hands of the established Congregational churches in the North and the Episcopalians in the South. Getting the state out of religious matters would be a boon to them. Distinguishing between their civil liberties and their quest for righteousness, most Baptists and Methodists endorsed Jefferson, who was actually a believing freethinker, because he had so crisply defined the differing domains of state and church.

The presidential campaign itself occupied the country from spring until the December convening of the Electoral College. Legislatures in six states chose their electors; seven states held popular at-large elections; and four had popular elections with voting in districts. The Federalists still disdained party organization and thus gave the edge to Republicans, who formed a campaign committee, led by a congressman, in each of the seventeen states. In Massachusetts, which the Republicans carried despite Federalist domination of the legislature, they engineered campaign activity at the level of wards. Geared to grand public ceremonies, the Republicans added a celebration of the anniversary of Jefferson's first inauguration to the regular July Fourth event. Philadelphia Republicans marked the anniversary of the Louisiana Purchase with parades of professional men, mechanics, and members of various benevolent societies—the St. Patrick's Society, the United Germany Benefit Society, and the "Young Men of Democratic Principles," each carrying an identifying banner. Despite Jefferson's cost-cutting in the navy, the expeditions against the Barbary pirates had produced victories, which Republicans celebrated with events in honor of Commodore Edward Preble and Captain Stephen Decatur.

For their part, the Federalists memorialized Washington's birthday as a way of establishing their auspicious origins. Their living heroes were Chief Justice John Marshall and Judge Samuel Chase. They were clearly on the defensive, and their attacks on Jefferson exceeded the limits of credibility: he aimed at a dictatorship; he patterned the Louisiana Territory after Napoleonic conquests; his informality at the White House threatened diplomatic relations with Great Britain. All this was accompanied by shrill criticism of Jefferson's alleged atheism, his dalliance with female slaves, and his utter rashness in trying to democratize the American republic. Both parties relied on partisan newspapers to carry their message, the stiffness and formality of the Federalist newspapers offering a sharp contrast to Republican populist prose.

Jefferson carried every state except Connecticut and Delaware, winning 162 electors to the Federalists' 14. This landslide made it considerably harder for the Federalists to view the democratic wave that carried Jefferson to victory as an aberration. The Republicans' triumph drove home the point that democratic rhetoric was not just a screen for Southern slaveholders, but resonated loudly among ordinary men, South and North. For his part, Jefferson was thrilled, writing to a friend, the French philosopher C. F. C. de Volney, that the two parties had almost wholly melted into one. With the stalwarts of the Federalist party, Washington and Hamilton, now dead, Adams rusticating at home in Braintree, Massachusetts, and Burr detested by everyone, Jefferson might have expected smooth sailing ahead. It was not to be. Foreign and domestic troubles soon collided, producing more friction and criticism in the next four years than Jefferson or the nation had bargained for.

At the peak of his popularity, in 1804, Jefferson led a people who shared fewer and fewer of his personal tastes. Reelected by a margin rarely equaled in American history, he secured a solid democratic base for the nation, but in other ways the country was moving away from the chaste political values Jefferson drew from the Enlightenment. The Second Great Awakening, which began with a series of phenomenally successful revivals in 1798, reshaped American Christianity. Powerful preachers pulled ordinary people, black and white, into a dense new circuit of meetings and services devoted to born-again proselytizing. Thousands responded to the insistent demand for an awakening to God. Temperance and Sabbatarianism became the public issues of the next decade, neither amenable to the Jeffersonian spirit of freedom. At sixty-three, Jefferson was an iconic figure from the Revolution presiding over a nation with a mean age of sixteen whose most commonly cherished goal was personal piety.

Money, reputation, and social prominence would never be negligible factors in American electoral politics, but no political party would ever again gain the presidency by arguing that the nation's leaders should come from families of established wealth and social prominence. Samuel Goodrich, who grew up in the bosom of such a family, claimed that the Federalist party was finally overthrown because "the great body of the people had got possession of suffrage, and insisted, with increasing vehemence, upon the removal of every impediment to its universality." Democracy became "the watchword of popular liberty" and permitted "the radical or republican party" to attract, among others, "the great body of the European immigrants—little instructed in our history or institutions."[6] Aggressive campaigning, ignorance of traditional wisdom, receptivity to newcomers in politics—these became the crude instruments that shattered the circle of virtue envisioned by Timothy Dwight.

Traditional values were undermined by the geographic mobility and material abundance that had become manifest in the United States by 1804. Hindsight, however, writes a premature obituary for the Federalists, for they continued to vie for office for another three decades. In 1808, they put up candidates for every single congressional seat north of the Potomac River, and they continued to do well in state elections through the 1820s, winning their last governorship in Delaware in 1823. Jefferson died in 1826 fearing their resurgence. Still, the deferential order the Federalists stood for had collapsed, and the Jeffersonians held on to the presidency through the next quarter-century—by which time democracy had found a new champion, in Andrew Jackson.

5

Contest for the West

The biggest story of the 1804 political campaign was not Jefferson's stunning victory over the Federalists, but the playing out of a rivalry far more deadly: that between Burr and Hamilton. The fatal end of their enmity prompted Burr to go west, with disastrous results for both him and Jefferson. Both men overreached: Burr in his ambition for glory, Jefferson in his determination to punish his errant vice president. Brought back to Richmond to stand trial for treason, Burr got unexpected help from the presiding judge, Chief Justice Marshall. The easy years of Jefferson's presidency were over, but he prevailed in the West, where the most vigorous opposition came from Native Americans struggling to keep their land.

New York politics drew Burr and Hamilton inexorably toward the dueling grounds. After being denied a second vice presidential race, Burr decided to run for the governorship of New York. His only chance of winning was to pick up Federalist support. And it was forthcoming, through Timothy Pickering, the Federalist leader in Congress. With more energy than good sense, Pickering was promoting a rogue plot to get New England to withdraw from the union and form a new confederation, which the Federalists could dominate. In return for Federalist votes in New York, Pickering hoped to induce Burr, once he became governor, to join the New England states in secession. In the event, Burr lost the election, and the plot evaporated.

Burr's defeat cooled talk of secession, but it convinced Hamilton of Burr's utter lack of scruples. Probably the only view that Hamilton and Jefferson shared these years was their assessment of Aaron Burr as a reckless adventurer unfit for public office. During the gubernatorial campaign, Burr got wind that Hamilton had made some unpleasant observations about his character. Hostility, pride, and defeat's quickened sense of honor prompted him to challenge Hamilton to a duel. The challenge signaled the beginning of an exquisite pas de deux; but unlike a dancing couple, both principals here wanted to lead. In his first letter to Hamilton, Burr cited a conversation in which Hamilton had traduced him. It had allegedly taken place the previous February, when congressional Republicans were dumping Burr. Instead of ending the affair with a nonspecific apology, Hamilton moved forward with his own aggressive step, informing Burr that he could not possibly be accountable for whatever others inferred from comments he had made about a political opponent over many years.

Although both were just shy of fifty, Hamilton and Burr responded with the arrogance and hostility of hotheaded youths, escalating their demands and firming their stubbornness through several exchanges of letters. After four weeks of negotiation, a date was set. On the morning of July 11, accompanied by seconds and a doctor, they rowed across the Hudson in separate boats, arranging themselves for their last go-round on a secluded ledge outside Weehawken, New Jersey. When given the signal, Hamilton missed, whether accidentally or deliberately, leaving Burr to take aim at five paces and end the dance with a fatal shot through Hamilton's rib cage.

Hamilton's death provoked an outpouring of grief at his very public funeral at Trinity Church. For his part, Burr received an avalanche of invective in his home state. He fled to Georgia to escape arrest after being indicted for murder in both New Jersey and New York.

One might well wonder what these self-conscious advocates of republican values were doing fighting a duel at all. The *code duello* was part of the aristocratic mores that Americans had spurned. It was in Europe that leisured men—particularly army officers—protected their honor with avidity and pistols. Dueling had not figured in colonial society. Gentlemen then cared about their honor, but they had not embraced the elaborate rituals of dueling to protect it, not until their exposure to the Europeans who came to fight in the Revolution. Just why dueling then became popular with the American gentry—it was a gentleman's privileged activity—remains something of a mystery. The more curious phenomenon is the rapid linkage of politics and duels. In the United States dueling throve on partisan warfare, an incongruous accompaniment to participatory politics.

Neither the pamphleteering before the Revolution nor the exchanges about the Constitution had prepared this generation of leaders for the vituperation of partisan disputes. The sudden emergence of parties had exposed American officeholders to attacks on their opinions and decisions at the very same time that the new national government created its own catch basin of publicity. The Constitution had created both a central government and a national electorate attuned to what that government was doing. This expanded arena of public attention multiplied the occasions when partisan vilification could put a gentleman's honor at risk. Nor did most of those involved in politics feel that they could refuse a challenge, even as they deplored the barbaric practice by which two otherwise rational men discharged firearms at each other at close range.

Americans even contributed an innovation to the dueling code with "postings." General James Wilkinson started the practice after Virginia's tempestuous and strong-willed congressional leader, John Randolph, ignored his challenge to a duel. When Congress reconvened, Wilkinson posted insulting notices at taverns and street corners all over the capital. The practice caught on. Soon newspapers became the principal conduit for postings, besides keeping up their role in broadcasting the opinions and remarks that might enrage opponents. The widespread publicizing of disputes, given peculiar force when printed, fanned the flames of animosity. A South Carolina journalist maintained that "three-fourths of the duels which have been fought in the United States were produced by political disputes," but he saw no relief, because "party violence is carried to an abominable excess."

When Vice President Burr slew Hamilton on the dueling grounds of Weehawken that summer of 1804, it was not the first—and was far from the last—of the political duels fought by Americans, Northern and Southern, in the first decades of the nineteenth century. Hamilton himself had had ten previous brushes with challenges, one of them with James Monroe. His son had died the year before in a duel precipitated when he mocked the speech of a Jeffersonian. A Wilmington newspaper estimated that more than a hundred men had lost their lives in duels in the first twenty years of the century.

In 1802, a Virginia congressman proposed appointing a committee to inquire whether it would be expedient to disqualify duelers from holding government office, but the measure failed to attract support. Four years later, Congress prohibited army officers from sending challenges to other officers, but congressmen continued to duel one another. Richard Dobbs Spaight, a prominent Virginia politician and signer of the Declaration of Independence, was killed in a duel prompted by a heated congressional campaign, and Jefferson's son-in-law Thomas Mann Randolph, infuriated by a trivial debate over a salt tax, as much as challenged John Randolph on the floor of Congress!

Eliza Quincy, wife of a Massachusetts congressman, wrote a friend from Washington in 1809 that the town was abuzz with talk of a duel between a Federalist from North Carolina and the jurist John George Jackson, who was James Madison's brother-in-law. Another duel a few days earlier, she reported, had taken the life of a young man of seventeen, and people feared that another dispute between the president's secretary and a member of Congress might end in the same way. "What a state of manners and morals," Quincy exclaimed.

Unable either to rein in their rhetoric in debate or to accept a slash-and-burn style of party politics, Congress became the spawning ground for many a duel. Most were held in nearby Bladensburg, Maryland, at a spot designated the congressional dueling ground. Editors editorialized, preachers preached, and college presidents inveighed, but the personal nature of partisan attacks, mixed with exaggerated notions about a man's need to defend his honor with violence, kept dueling alive. Public opinion held that no man who was not conspicuously religious could refuse a challenge.

Age and temperament also played a part. Neither George Washington, Thomas Jefferson, nor James Madison was ever involved in a challenge or response, yet they were in the thick of the partisan battles. Fearful of these murderous acts of wounded pride, Jefferson implored his grandson never to fight to defend his grandfather's reputation, because, as he explained, it lay "in the hands of my fellow citizens at large, and will be consigned to honor or infamy by the verdict of the republican mass of our country, according to what themselves will have seen, not what their enemies and mine shall have said."

Agonizing for Jefferson was the intemperate response of his son-in-law to the insinuations of John Randolph. Frantic to keep the news of the spat from his daughter, Jefferson sent a secret letter to her husband. Knowing well his thin skin, Jefferson assured him that he would not ask that anything be done that might "lessen you in the esteem of the world." Trying to calm the young man down, he advised correcting false statements and cautioned him that the "least expression of passion on the one side draws forth a little more of the other, and ends at last in the most barbarous of appeals." Then, weighing the two sides in a way that reveals both his contempt of John Randolph and his anxiety for his daughter, he urged his son-in-law to consider the differences in what the prospective duelers had at stake: "On his side, unentangled in the affections of the world, a single life, of no value to himself or others. On yours, yourself, a wife, & a family of children, all depending for all their happiness & protection in this world on you alone."[1] Happily, good sense prevailed, as it failed to do between Burr and Hamilton.

Though the papers could not say enough about Hamilton's agonizing death or Burr's ignominious flight, Jefferson never commented on the affair in his voluminous correspondence. How strange it must have seemed to him to have a dubious political ally slay his most serious political rival, the lodestar of the Federalist party. One can't but wonder what difference it would have made for Jefferson's presidency if Hamilton had slain Burr and not Burr Hamilton.

Burr managed to evade the warrants for his arrest and returned to Washington for the remaining months of his vice presidential term, where he presided over the trial of Samuel Chase. The people who packed the Senate for this trial marveled at Burr's dignity, composure, and sagacity, even though his presence there as presiding officer had elicited a cutting remark from a Federalist wag: formerly, he said, it had been the practice "to arraign the murderer before the judge, but now we behold the judge arraigned before the murderer." When Burr's term ended in early 1805, he found himself burdened with a life unburdened with official responsibilities. Having demolished his political prospects in the United States, he showed just how resilient he was by launching himself as a grand strategist in the turbulent West of the early nineteenth century.

Twenty-first-century Americans may look upon the political map of the United States as it overlies the physical features of the continent with a confidence that this is how it was meant to be. We can be indifferent to the struggle it took to gain the nation its ocean-to-ocean borders. When Burr took his leave of the Senate with an eloquent address in March 1805, three European powers were pursuing expansive policies in North America. Since the sixteenth century, European countries had treated the islands, rivers, and valleys of the North American continent like so many chess pieces to be moved about on their negotiating boards. The Spanish still maintained a presence in Florida and Mexico, the British in Canada. France had sold Louisiana, but the Mississippi Valley was dotted with French settlers, who might be successfully wooed by the proper suitor. And, of course, most of the Native American tribes still lived on ancestral lands, which they were prepared to fight to keep. The eighteenth-century diplomacy of Europe had revealed to all just how tenuous borders were, just how dizzying could be the exchange of huge chunks of continental real estate through the simple gesture of signing yet another peace treaty.

Into this thicket of intrigues came Burr with a plan to detach the western states from the Union. He actually approached Merry, the British ambassador, for help with this grandiose scheme while still vice president—confirming, if they had known it, Jefferson's and Hamilton's shared estimate of the man. Burr found the perfect partner in perfidy in James Wilkinson, the commanding general of the U.S. Army, he who hounded Randolph with his insulting "postings." One can only guess at the power of Wilkinson's charm, given the fact that Presidents Washington, Adams, and Jefferson showered him with appointments and promotions during a career pockmarked with dubious speculations, nasty vendettas, and duplicitous bargains.

After fighting in the Continental Army, Wilkinson went to Kentucky to repair his fortunes. There he tapped into the discontents of similarly restless men. Mobilizing volunteers to fight the Shawnees in 1791, Wilkinson got his army commission back. He became the nation's ranking general in 1796, after the unexpected death of his superior, and spent the next decade traveling throughout the French, Spanish, English, and U.S. outposts that dotted the international boundaries of the West. Chronically short of money, he spied for the Spanish, who made him a permanent pensioner. His travels convinced him that most residents of the West could be lured into a new political unit by an intrepid leader.

Every inch a rogue, Wilkinson offered Burr firsthand information about the West as well as insider knowledge of the various combinations of schemers seeking personal benefit from the rivalries roiling the frontier. To follow the trail Burr blazed across the frontier is to discover the myriad of plots, fantastic dreams, and international rivalries that unsettled the unsettled part of the nation. Burr and

Wilkinson apparently began with discussions about an invasion of Mexico, an attack somehow connected to the larger design of forming a new country from the disaffected groups in Kentucky, Tennessee, and the territories. Since it was in the interest of the European powers to halt the advance of the United States, Burr's initial forays into covert diplomacy could be expected to meet with some success.

Soon this thorn in Jefferson's side turned into a plunging dagger, which the president extricated at great cost to his reputation for fairness. The West was full of rumors that found their way East. A Federalist newspaper in Philadelphia ran a series of "Queries" about whether Burr intended to invade Mexico or form a separate government in the West. An anonymous letter-writer warned Jefferson in December 1805 that Burr had become a British pensioner; then a federal official in Kentucky wrote asserting that General Wilkinson, who had just been named governor of Louisiana, was in the pay of Spain. Western informants told so many different stories linking the names of Wilkinson and Burr with assorted adventurers that the reports began to lose credibility. No one knew exactly what Burr was planning, and whatever it was, he wasn't sharing his plans with the president. The government faced something of a catch-22. The Constitution specified that a treason conviction required two witnesses "to the same overt act" of levying war or adhering or giving aid and comfort to an enemy, but allowing such an overt act to take place might well endanger the country.

Warnings of Burr's escapades in the West continued throughout 1806, taking away some of "the unspeakable joy" Jefferson reported feeling on receiving word that Lewis and Clark, with all but one of their men, had returned safely to St. Louis. During the fall, Burr had gathered supplies, boats, and men for what looked like a descent on New Orleans launched from an island near Marietta, Ohio. Perhaps because he was still the highest-ranking officer in the Army, Wilkinson got cold feet and leaked details of the scheme. Local officials moved in on Burr, arresting him three different times, but without winning convictions. Burr at this point became fearful that

his association with Wilkinson might lead to a court-martial. Word
of Jefferson's wrath may also have reached him. He set off for
Mobile but was apprehended on the way and brought back to Richmond. The government arraigned him for treason before the Virginia Circuit Court in the spring of 1807, with John Marshall
presiding.

The hundred-day trial turned out to be one of the great spec-
tacles of the early republic: the former vice president defending
himself against charges of treason before the Chief Justice of the
United States. A star-studded cast of lawyers rushed to Richmond.

The gathering conspicuously displayed lawyers' newfound status as members of the most prestigious profession in the new
nation. Not only had staffing the country's dual judicial system and
serving as commissioners to deal with bankruptcies, estate auctions,
and the laying out of roads increased their numbers, but the pre-
dominance of politics in American life gave lawyers a degree of
influence previously enjoyed only by religious leaders. The Presbyterian Lyman Beecher complained that lawyers had displaced cler-
gymen as interpreters of public events. And the Burr trial was a
public event that needed interpreting. Past and future senators, gov-
ernors, and judges crowded the galleries, just to watch their colleagues perform; Burr himself exerted a magnetic appeal.

Only the president was absent from the trial, but absence did
not indicate inattention. The ferocity of Jefferson's outrage at Burr's
conduct fueled the prosecution. No friend of the presiding judge
either, Jefferson must have had some intimation of the difficulties
that lay ahead when he learned that Marshall had attended a pre-
trial dinner party where Burr was in attendance. Further to stir ugly
passions, the last volume of Marshall's *Life of Washington* appeared
shortly before the trial began. It was in this volume that Marshall
described the origins of the political movement that had formed
in opposition to his hero. As Jefferson confided in his memoirs
later, Marshall depicted the Republicans as "a mere set of grum-
blers, and disorganizers, satisfied with no government, without
fixed principles."[2]

There is something fascinating about the conjunctions among the careers of Marshall, Hamilton, Burr, and Jefferson. A man with few personal enemies—partisan opponents excepted—Jefferson must have wondered at the peculiar way these three nemeses of his interacted. Burr had cleared Hamilton from the political scene, but simultaneously turned him into a martyr, and now Marshall was poised to redeem Burr from the charge of treason.

Despite what Jefferson considered indisputable evidence that Burr was plotting against his country, the former vice president again eluded conviction, and of course he always denied that he had ever plotted disunion. It was not an easy case to prosecute, and the defense team adroitly outwitted the government. Marshall narrowed the definition of treason sufficiently to get Burr off.

In a way the government had stymied itself: in stopping what appeared to be treasonable activities that put the country's relations with Spain at risk, officials had interfered with the very activities that would have proved the treason charge. When authorities seized the boats readied for the descent down the Mississippi, they scuttled their own case. Nor did their chief witness, Wilkinson, help, for he had to incriminate himself as an erstwhile conspirator in order to testify against Burr. Marshall's rulings made treason a difficult charge to prove and hence ineffective as a purely political weapon. But the trial did remove the troublemaking Burr from the American scene. The following June, he left for Europe, returning after four years, when his notoriety had dissipated, to resume his New York law practice.

Jefferson had many reasons for hating Burr, but his obsession with convicting him of treason—the punishment would have been execution—stemmed in part from his own long love affair with the West where Burr was a Johnny-come-lately, more intent upon reclaiming personal power than on fulfilling a national dream. Everything visionary in Jefferson's plans for America sprang from his hope to create a new world in the New World, to show Europeans that men could fend for themselves without hierarchical structures of church and state. No such high-minded or even far-sighted purpose ennobled Burr's schemes, and that fact made him more treacherous and more contemptible in Jefferson's eyes. Jefferson's sense of personal rectitude may have blinded him to his own defects, but it certainly enhanced his perception of others'.

White Americans, thriving under the reign of liberty and equality, would give substance to the philosophy of natural rights. Where better than the sparsely populated West to prove the possibility of a peaceful society of self-regulating families, loosely joined in political association, living harmoniously as they pursued their own goals. Such a demonstration would retrieve human nature from the gloomy reflections of conservatives and give a realistic footing to democracy.

The peace treaty that ended the War of Independence had ceded to the United States the exclusive privilege of negotiating with the tribes in the area between the Appalachian Mountains and the Mississippi River. However, the peace treaty did not *give* the land to the United States, as is often said, because no one signing the peace treaty had control of that land and the Native Americans who lived there—the Illinois, Pawnee, Sioux, Shawnees, Wynandots, and Miami—gave plenty of evidence of their intention of holding on to their ancestral homes. Wresting territory from them was not going to be easy.

The new citizens of the United States carried with them old attitudes toward indigenous peoples. Jefferson's birthplace, Charlottesville, was close to the Virginia frontier; his father had been a pioneer of Albemarle County. Growing up among the planter elite of Virginia, Jefferson himself had plenty of experience with colonial efforts to push settlement into Indian territory. Officials in seventeenth-century Virginia had been the first to set up reservations for dispossessed Indians. With the population growth of the eighteenth century, the seemingly empty spaces of the West quickened the imagination of Virginia planters, George Washington among them. They acquired the skills of surveying, that quintessential European tool for impressing geographical notation upon raw land in preparation for its conversion from the natural to the social.

Virginia land speculation had triggered the French and Indian War of 1754–63, which in turn unleashed a succession of surprise attacks on American settlements along the frontier. Stories dramatizing barbaric Indian practices abounded during Jefferson's adolescence. The frequent description of Indians as barbaric calls to mind Voltaire's quip about the dog: a species so vicious that, if attacked, it would bite. In the months before Independence, Virginia's last royal governor launched another Indian war, an act that may have inspired Jefferson's line in the Declaration of Independence charging the king with fomenting "domestic insurrections amongst us," by inciting "the merciless Indian Savages." Talk of fighting the Indians absorbed the energies of young Virginians, who could not have imagined that their descendants might one day condemn their belligerence toward the native inhabitants of the continent.

The idea that the United States would become a continental nation surfaced quickly. Thomas Paine in *Common Sense* had derided the notion that a mere island like Great Britain should rule a continent. This thrilled the restive colonists but hardly conformed to the reality that the thirteen colonies were actually perched on the Atlantic shelf of the continent they presumed to possess. Intention triumphed over reality. Although delegates to the first meeting of colonial representatives decided to call their gathering a Congress, popular usage soon added "Continental" to the title. Whether this expectation of westward expansion came from the original sea-to-sea charters or grew with the relative ease of dispossessing Indians is hard to say, but independence only strengthened the notion of a continental destiny for white settlers.

The Revolution had created new opportunities for advancing American claims in Indian territory. As wartime governor of Virginia, Jefferson enthusiastically endorsed the ambitious western campaign of the revolutionary frontier leader George Rogers Clark. Working with Jefferson's predecessor, Patrick Henry, Clark explored the possibility of detaching the French settlements along the Mississippi from Great Britain. These clusters of Indian traders and fur trappers had come under British rule when France gave up its

North American possessions at the close of the French and Indian War in 1763. Hardly likely to feel any loyalty to France's ancient enemy, they in fact renounced their ties to Great Britain once Clark captured the posts of Kaskaskia and Vincennes. Clark's success offered concrete proof that an independent America could challenge Britain's dominance of the Ohio and Mississippi valleys.

Europeans had also convinced themselves that they were fitter to settle the continent than its existing population. They set great store by their culture's technological advances and their own personal habits of relentless and disciplined effort. Watching the Indians oscillate between periods of intense application and extended idleness, Americans came to think of them as childlike. (Ethnic pride worked both ways. Some of the Cherokees told an American official that they were not of the same stock as white men, and that the Great Spirit did not intend them to lead the laborious lives of Europeans.) Innocent as mere ethnocentric observations, such views provided rationalizations for expelling the native inhabitants from the coveted valleys beyond the Appalachian Mountains.

By the time he had to craft an Indian policy as president, Jefferson had given much thought to the indigenous peoples of the continent. Native American languages had earlier aroused his curiosity. His *Notes on the State of Virginia* brought together personal experience with the prevailing anthropological knowledge about Native Americans. A polemic bubbled just beneath the surface of his commentary: Jefferson was intent on refuting the French naturalist Buffon, who claimed that flora and fauna deteriorated over time in North America. Buffon's popularizers outdid the philosopher in their pessimism about natural developments in the Western Hemisphere. They cultivated the notion that the debilitating climate of the New World would have its effect on European settlers. Benjamin Franklin, who like Jefferson was tall, used a parlor trick to mock the idea. When a dinner-party conversation turned to Buffon's theories, Franklin invited all present to rise and compare their heights, so as to judge for themselves, on the spot, which environment might be considered debilitating. Jefferson sustained a more serious line of criticism, as was his wont. He tracked Buffon through all his principal points, arguing for the similarities in the European and American environment.

Once a federal government had been established, Native Americans began to receive more sustained attention from officials of the United States. Congress authorized Christian missionaries to proselytize among Indians confined to reservations. Without a direct debate on the subject, policymakers assumed a kind of benevolent tyranny over the continent's native population. Transforming that population became a public undertaking. The question of how the Indians might change was caught up in a philosophical argument about the human capacity for development. Washington's secretary of war, Henry Knox, bemoaned the fact that Indians from the thirteen original states had never been taught agriculture. Such reflections suggested that the officials of the new United States might do for the tribes west of the Appalachians what their English forebears had failed to do in their seventeenth-century encounters.

These arguments complicated matters for Jefferson, but he never allowed his intellectual interests to take precedence over his determination to plant American institutions in the fertile soil of the West. He made that clear when he wrote Clark during the Revolution that if America was to wage war against the Indians, "the end proposed should be their extermination, or their removal beyond the lakes of Illinois river. The same world will scarcely do for them and us." When he became president, Jefferson followed the practice of his predecessors and bought land from Indian tribes whenever possible. He shrewdly deployed American forces to protect the routes of the inland trade that Americans pursued alongside the British, who had not yet abandoned their Great Lakes posts, the French settlers, and the Spanish, who then held Louisiana. He encouraged Americans to settle close to contested borders to bolster the militias called upon to help the army defend American territory.

Jefferson's unflagging curiosity was alerted when he learned that Napoleon was offering to sell the whole vast unexplored area of

Louisiana. He peppered with questions anyone who knew anything about its flora, fauna, geography, history, laws, or native occupants, including the French and Spanish denizens of New Orleans. In 1802, he secured secret congressional approval to send Meriwether Lewis and William Clark on an exploratory expedition into the Upper Louisiana. The Lewis and Clark expedition—it combined Indian diplomacy, commercial prospecting, scientific investigation, and military reconnaissance—captured the imagination of the whole country, promising to provide fascinating detail about the terrain that Jefferson had called "an empire for liberty." He was equally eager for American traders to woo Native American tribes away from European rivals, and he outlined this policy in letters to William Henry Harrison, who was then governor of Indiana Territory and superintendent of Indian affairs. Ever the long-range planner, he sent off Lewis and Clark with detailed instructions about treating with the Indians beyond the Mississippi. He even had medals made to be handed out to the Indians they encountered, as a way of aligning these tribes of the far West to the United States.

Among the many tribes that Lewis and Clark encountered, the Osages and Mandans were the most impressive. Lewis had extended an invitation to the Osage nation to send a delegation to Washington to meet the president. Jefferson rejoiced to discover the men's considerable height, no doubt thinking of his protracted challenge to Buffon's theory of New World degeneracy. Like all the early presidents, Jefferson welcomed the Indians with fulsome assurances of good feeling that make one wince in the reading: "We are all now of one family, born in the same land, & bound to live as brothers. . . . The great Spirit has given you strength, and has given us strength, not that we might hurt one another, but to do each other all the good in our power."[3]

The presidency gave Jefferson a large canvas upon which to paint his picture of Indian-white relations. As a thinker imbued with the Enlightenment conviction that European men of science had opened up a totally new era in the history of mankind, he looked upon Native Americans as backward. The very word suggested a framework for understanding human experience in which a few favored groups were in the vanguard of progress with the rest of humankind trapped in pockets of suspended development. Condescension was the only attitude possible for those with this perspective, as Jefferson demonstrated in his repeated efforts to lure Indians away from their economy of hunting and gathering and into the sedentary—and hence more civilized—economy of farming.

In the early part of his administration, Jefferson pursued a more or less benign policy of encouraging Indians to join the march of progress. Unlike Africans, Indians could incorporate themselves into the nation if they wished. Jefferson was even willing to pursue a dubious policy to lure Indians to adopt an agrarian way of life by letting Indians who traded with Americans run up a debt, which could then be most easily extinguished by trading large tracts of hunting land for smaller farm parcels. This Jefferson justified by the conviction that tribal living was doomed to destruction, one way or the other. The Louisiana Purchase made even more urgent a settling with the Indians. When most of them proved indifferent to appeals to change their ways, Jefferson saw confirmation that they were savages who had been bypassed by history's progress.

Time told against a civilizing program, and Americans were in a hurry. In his second inaugural address, Jefferson somewhat disingenuously used the Native Americans' dwindling land base as an urgent reason for change: "[H]umanity enjoins us to teach them agriculture and the domestic arts; to encourage them to that industry which alone can enable them to maintain their place in existence." Explaining that the United States government had liberally supplied Indians with the tools for a sedentary way of life, he denounced the traditionalists among them for inculcating "a sanctimonious reverence for the customs of their ancestors." This was exactly what he thought to be true of his domestic opponents, the Federalists.

In these forays into nation-building in the West, Americans continued the propulsive forward motion that Europeans in the New World had embarked upon in the fifteenth century. In his enthusiasm for westward expansion, Jefferson was no different from many other American leaders. To the continental ambitions of the United States, he brought his characteristic persistence, meticulous planning, and tenacity. He never lost sight of his goal: a continent filled with a people speaking the same language, governed in similar forms and by similar laws. As he noted ominously in a letter to Virginia's governor, James Monroe, written shortly after he became president, we can not "contemplate with satisfaction, either blot or mixture" on the continent. After the Louisiana Purchase, Jefferson began to contemplate removal of the Indians as an alternative to civilizing them.

This Jeffersonian view of Western prosperity and freedom applied only to ordinary white men, whose innate worth had been maligned by generations of gentlemen. Smashing the barriers erected to segregate the highborn few from the humble many was the social reform that turned Jefferson into a zealot. When he spoke of all men being endowed by their creator with certain inalienable rights, his words challenged the received political faith that the world was divided between the excellent, brave, wise, talented few, and the many capable only of living lives of drudgery. Race and culture were less salient for white Americans than the venerable distinctions of birth and status. Jefferson's hopes for a new future simply ignored Africans and Indians. A categorical prejudice against them undermined the nobility of his dream. In all probability he had never seen them behave as the autonomous individuals his theory required.

No less implacable as president than he had been twenty years earlier as Virginia's governor, Jefferson reacted angrily when he heard that the two great Shawnee leaders, Tecumseh and his brother, the prophet Tenskwatawa, were urging their tribesmen not to sell any land. Alerted to the possibility that the Shawnees might play off the United States against the British in the Great Lakes area, Jefferson wrote his secretary of war that the Indians should be told that if the United States must ever "lift the hatchet against any tribe, we will never lay it down till the tribe is exterminated, or driven beyond the Mississippi." Menacingly he warned that while "they will kill some of us; we shall destroy all of them." Despite this harsh stance, Jefferson refused to arrest Tenskwatawa because he considered such an act inimical to the rules by which the American government should operate.

In working diligently to devise ways of expelling the Native Americans from the trans-Appalachian West, Jefferson was putting himself in tune with the desires of ordinary white Americans, who poured into the West whenever peace permitted safe passage. Two astute European visitors, one in 1797, the other twenty years later, left graphic pictures of Americans' restlessness. The Duc de La Rochefoucauld-Liancourt encountered farmers moving on to some other place at every tavern he stayed at in the rural areas of New England, Pennsylvania, and New York. He asked whether American farmers shared the French peasant's attachment to a particular piece of ground. His American listeners told him, he reported, that such fixity of place revealed a certain lack of pluck. The United States, he concluded, was "a country in flux." "That which is true today as regards its population, its establishments, its prices, its commerce," he stressed, "will not be true six months from now."[4]

Morris Birkbeck, writing for his English compatriots, considered it almost impossible to convey to others the American love of movement. Imagine, he wrote, the numerous stagecoaches, light wagons, and horseback riders and "you have before you a scene of bustle and business, extending over a space of three hundred miles, which is truly wonderful."[5] The mobility of young adults leaving the places of their birth, the mobility of talent searching for its optimal rewards, or the mobility of cash and credit chasing after enterprise conspired to keep all in La Rochefoucauld's flux.

For Jefferson, the West did not evoke schemes for dismembering the United States as Burr had contemplated, but an empire of liberty—white men's liberty, free of European hierarchies and backward races, a place of new beginnings, a tabula rasa for the American Adam, that self-sufficient, liberty-loving, energetic innovator supported by his independent family. He and his ilk would carry the plow, the church, the schoolroom, and the courthouse into the fertile land that had heretofore been the haunts of savages. Nature's order took on a real, literal quality for Americans, as it hardly could for Europeans. When Americans turned and looked west they confronted millions of acres as yet uncultivated in the European style, a vast virgin land upon which to inscribe enlightened social practices. Jefferson explicitly detached liberty for them from its ancient Spartan linkage to self-denial, and reattached it to the promise of prosperity. His optimism floated on expectations of material abundance. The goals he articulated as president required the expanding frontier west of the Appalachian Mountains. Without land, men could not achieve personal autonomy. In the vast lands of the West lay what no other country had ever possessed—a material base for a growing citizenry of independent, industrious property holders.

6

———

Foreign Policy Proves a Quagmire

Jefferson premised his foreign policy goals on principle, but in clearing a path for American expansion he willingly took a detour through the duplicities of diplomacy. He was temperamentally peace-loving, but his yearning to see white families spread across the continent trumped his aversion to violence, or at least permitted him to threaten it. Jefferson coined the phrase about avoiding "foreign entanglements," usually attributed to Washington, yet his presidential ambitions drew him ever more deeply into international parleys. And, as in a good play, a voice emerged to taunt him for these inconsistencies.

Jefferson had been tormented during Adams's administration when it looked as if the Federalists' bellicosity would plunge the nation into war with France. His opponents mocked his moderating tendencies as unmanly. Never mind: his longing to cut taxes bolstered his craving for peace. Without a military buildup there would be no need for more revenue. All would have been well had Jefferson also not wanted to settle Americans across the North American continent. To achieve this bold objective would require foreign allies, not to mention compromises made to secure them. To create an "empire of liberty" and spread American institutions beyond the Mississippi, Jefferson was willing to prevaricate, deceive, and deal.

Other pitfalls endangered the president's moves on the global theater. Jefferson considered foreign policy his forte, but he refused to play the conventional game. What he wanted for the United States ran athwart the established practices of Europe's major powers. Not content just to serve the national interest, Jefferson aspired to set new standards for a world indifferent to transcendent values. When he became chief executive of America's diplomacy in 1801, his grandiose plans to expand the realm of human freedom became policy goals. Unswerving in his commitment to high principles, he steered his presidential foreign policy onto the shoals of doctrinaire obduracy more than once. And when Jefferson did swerve from the path of virtue, he rarely acknowledged it, twisting himself into a pretzel to justify national interests that needed no justification among amoral diplomats.

Although Jefferson expressed his policies in the sonorous universals of natural law, we can see now that they were ethnocentric in design and spirit. Stirred by the loftiness of his ideals, he seemed oblivious to the fact that planting American institutions across the plains would obliterate the Indian cultures that had flourished there for generations. He seemed equally indifferent to the fact that his empowering of ordinary white men left ordinary black men with more masters and less freedom. The universal truths he spoke for bore the traces of a particular philosophical position. In such contradictions, most of his contemporaries were equally blind, but no other figure articulated Americans' sentiments in such elegant phrasing, so it has been Jefferson called to the bar of history for the white supremacist basis of American foreign policy.

When he first became involved in diplomacy, as minister to France and the nation's first secretary of state, Jefferson was the very embodiment of an innocent abroad. But, as is the way with innocence, it often sees things invisible to old eyes. His education was wrested from both experience and introspection, hope and despair. When he succeeded Benjamin Franklin in France in 1784, he was thrust into the thorny thickets of international commerce. With John Adams, minister to Great Britain, he assiduously promoted American trading interests, which he had previously understood through the narrow vision of a Southern planter. Charged with getting the best terms possible from America's creditors, the two diplomats also mastered the details of international finance.

Whitehall officials assumed that the United States would continue to need Britain's goods and goodwill, so they could afford to indulge their pique at their former colonies. Visiting England on his only trip to Europe, Jefferson had been enraptured by the remarkable new inventions that were transforming British industry and soon the world. They were as novel and pathbreaking, in his reckoning, as the government was hidebound. Zealous to achieve economic independence to match America's political autonomy, Jefferson tried to push American commerce toward France, but the pull of old trading patterns proved too strong. Although his efforts to redirect American trade proved unavailing, he did succeed in holding a censorious attitude toward Great Britain for the rest of his life.

From their respective posts in London and Paris, Adams and Jefferson got a preview of how the ferocious enmity between France and England affected everything from the price of tobacco to the flow of political news. Nothing revealed the hostility's long reach more than the startling disintegration of the French monarchy. Aiding England's rebellious American colonies had exhausted the French royal coffers, forcing the king to summon the old Estates, which hadn't met in more than 170 years. More than a concession to reformers, this set off the chain reaction that eventually brought Louis XVI to the guillotine. When the leaders of France's Third Estate, the bourgeoisie, succeeded in 1789 in transforming the meeting of the Estates into a modern national assembly, Jefferson's love of France grew boundless.

The excitement of these opening acts of the French Revolution intensified Jefferson's distaste for things British, a bias that was to influence his presidential foreign policy. In 1789, France provided him with an example of a moribund monarchy transformed into a model of civic virtue for the modern world. This he would hold up against the pettiness of British officials and Britons' slavish admiration of institutions just because they were old. The "National Assembly [of France] have now as clean a canvas to work on here as we had in America," he declared after the Assembly abolished aristocratic privilege and issued the Declaration of the Rights of Man and of the Citizen.

At a critical moment during the electric summer of 1789, the Marquis de Lafayette, a hero of the American Revolution, asked Jefferson to open his dining room to a high-level discussion among members of the National Assembly. Describing himself a "silent witness" during the six hours of debate that followed, Jefferson carried back home the next month an impression of candor and competency at France's helm. Alas, those gathered at the American minister's table that night were but the first in a succession of revolutionary leaders to be consumed by revolutionary flames before Napoleonic authoritarianism quenched the fire altogether.

Not unexpectedly, Jefferson and Adams gleaned different lessons from the French Revolution. Like the great English conservative Edmund Burke, Adams flinched at the cavalier destruction of established institutions in France. He seriously doubted that a nation that had just destroyed its church could possibly summon the virtue to rule itself. Jefferson found himself more in tune with Burke's adversary Thomas Paine. The two clashed in a famous exchange of pamphlets. To stir sympathy for the victims of the Revolution, Burke evoked the regal beauty of Queen Marie Antoinette, who had been forced from her quarters at Versailles by an angry crowd of Parisian poor. Weighed in Burke's scales their misery could not match or justify the indignity of dragging a queen from her palace. Paine famously retorted, "[H]e pities the plumage, but forgets the dying bird."

The United States was also going through a period of dramatic reform during those same years. In 1786–87, an uprising of Massachusetts farmers, led by the Continental Army veteran Daniel Shays, shocked American leaders as they prepared themselves to reform the Articles of Confederation, which had been holding the states together since the end of the war. Out of the Philadelphia Convention came a draft constitution, sent to the states to be voted up or down in thirteen ratifying conventions. With rare political equanimity, Americans debated a prospective form of government for the next nineteen months. This stunning show of stability prompted the celebrated hostess Madame d'Houdetot to comment to Jefferson that the "characteristic difference between your revolution and ours, is that having nothing to destroy, you had nothing to injure." "Every step in your revolution was perhaps the effect of virtue," she added, "while ours are often faults, and sometimes crimes." It was a sentiment that Jefferson and most Americans shared, preferring to ignore the cost of their revolution to the ravaged Native Americans or the contradiction implicit in a nation that was dedicated to freedom yet kept one in five of its people enslaved.

The future second and third presidents of the United States were more than a little frustrated at being so far from home while Americans deliberated about a new form of government. Shays's Rebellion inspired one of Jefferson's most famous metaphors—actually two of them. Abigail Adams, in a classic conservative response to protest, assailed Jefferson for not seeing that the debt-ridden farmers of Massachusetts were "ignorant, wrestles desperadoes, without conscience or principals" who had deluded a multitude "to follow their standard, under pretence of grievances which have no existence but in their immaginations." Jefferson calmly replied, "I like a little rebellion from time to time. It clears the atmosphere." A month later he proclaimed to another friend: "The tree of liberty must be refreshed from time to time with the blood of patriots and tyrants. It is its natural manure."[1]

When Adams and Jefferson received copies of the draft constitution, they rushed to exchange their opinions of its strengths and weaknesses. The Constitution's provisions for the presidency interested both of them, as well it might have. Having grown to manhood as subjects of George II and George III, they could not wholly detach themselves from the reference point of a king when they thought about executive power. However deficient hereditary monarchy might be in other ways, it had solved the vexing problem of transferring power. "The king is dead; long live the king!" crowds shouted when death delivered the throne to the heir apparent. The fact that the Constitution permitted the repeated reelection of the president troubled Jefferson, while the frequency of elections alarmed Adams. He evidently shared his wife's fear of the mobbish multitude and of anything that might catch its attention, such as an election.

One more influence from Jefferson's five-year stint in France shaped his presidential foreign policy. This was the "model treaty" carried to France by the American peace commissioners at the end of the War for Independence. The treaty had laid out a grand plan for global free trade, with acknowledgment of the rights of neutral countries in times of war. Haughtily rejected by the Europeans—Britain refused to consider making any kind of commercial treaty with its erstwhile colonies—the treaty set forth a distinctive set of American principles that Jefferson ardently embraced. By those principles, America's farming families might freely dispatch their crops around the world without fear of embroilment in the constant warfare among European monarchies. Agrarian self-sufficiency never appealed to Jefferson; he plumped instead for a rural prosperity built on the export of America's bumper crops.

It's in the nature of optimists to underestimate the difficulty of achieving their heart's desire. And Jefferson was the Revolution's optimist. Optimism was both the engine and the spanner in his foreign policy. It goaded him to push where no one had pushed before—as in his zealous advocacy of freedom of the seas—and it immobilized him when those grim realities that pessimists focus upon blocked his path. Jefferson feared war and avoided it whenever possible, but he became bellicose when others thwarted his plans. Europe had not signed on to the Americans' idealistic view of international relations. Federalists grasped this truth, but for Jefferson to do so would have been to dam the springs of his own resourcefulness. With his rose-tinted view of the world, he imagined that stupidity, greed, and revenge would yield eventually to reason and virtue. *Eventually,* of course, is a variable term, and eight years proved an insufficient time for virtue and reason to deliver on his goals. But Jefferson made free trade and continental expansion the twin pillars of Republican foreign policy. Treaties were appraised and trades promoted under their aegis.

The audacity of a minor country perched on the Atlantic shelf of the North American continent plotting to expel the French, Spanish, and British who had been in North America since the sixteenth century still induces awe. When Jefferson became president, fewer than six million people lived in the United States. They were scattered up and down the Atlantic Coast. The frontier line ran through the western parts of the thirteen original states. Kentucky, Tennessee, and Vermont had been added to the union; Ohio, the first state formed from the Northwest Territory, was about to enter (in 1803). Only New York, Philadelphia, Baltimore, and Boston had populations larger than 25,000. Yet few leaders in the United States doubted that they could and should plant American farms, schools, and courthouses across the West. In this, Jefferson headed a popular cause. Only with difficulty did he give up the idea of annexing Canada to the United States, and he persisted in considering Cuba for the same treatment. With equal forcefulness, Americans disputed the right of the indigenous people to retain their ancestral homes. Believing profoundly in the superiority of their civilization, Americans acted as though this capacity conferred legitimacy upon their insatiable desire for land.

By the beginning of the nineteenth century, one key piece of information bolstered the resolve of Americans to displace the Indian inhabitants: they knew that they could domesticate the wilderness. Their colonial forebears had virtually swept into oblivion the native tribes that had once lived along the Atlantic Coast. The citizens of the new country were equally prepared to risk being slain as intruders in the fight for access to the fertile acres that stretched westward beyond the Appalachian Mountains. Retrospectively it looks like a case of might making right, but Americans in the nineteenth century moved toward the setting sun without the shame that filled their descendants who are inclined to look back on the displacement of the Indians as acts of ethnic cleansing.

The leaders of the United States had dreamed of a continental destiny for three decades. The country had an army of settlers on the ground to oppose the designs on paper of European powers. With the labor of their burgeoning families, they could break sod and create complete communities within five years. As the last Spanish governor of Louisiana had said, the Americans were "advancing and multiplying in the silence of peace." Jefferson's determination to secure the continent for the white families of the United States represented but the audacious implementation of what had long been a general expectation. That he held it with the same intensity as the man on the frontier helps explain his pervasive popularity. No bewigged gentleman sat in the White House, detached from the dreams of his people. The successive expeditions sent out in relentless pursuit of information about the continent, and the steady buying up of Indian land in the Ohio River Valley, announced a collective will that was galvanized by a resolute leader and that would neither fade nor fail.

Americans were no less aggressive on the high seas. Alexis de Tocqueville, visiting the United States some years later, marveled at the contrast between the American and the European shipper. The latter, he noted "ventures on the seas only with prudence; he departs only when the weather invites him to; if an unforeseen accident comes upon him, he enters into port; at night he furls a part of his sails, and when he sees the ocean whiten at the approach of land, he slows his course and examines the sun. . . . The American neglects these precautions and braves the dangers." De Tocqueville continued:

> He departs while the tempest still roars; at night as in day he opens all his sails to the wind; while on the go, he repairs his ship, worn down by the storm, and when he finally approaches the end of his course, he continues to fly toward the shore as if he already perceived the port. The American is

often shipwrecked; but there is no navigator who crosses the seas as rapidly as he does. Doing the things as another in less time, he can do them at less expense. . . . I cannot express my thoughts better than by saying that the Americans put a sort of heroism into their manner of doing commerce.[2]

News of Lewis and Clark's safe return in October 1806 capped the triumph of the Louisiana Purchase. In many ways this was the high point of Jefferson's presidency. Lewis and Clark had found the headwaters of the Missouri, reached the Pacific, made contact with many new Indian tribes, scouted out the commercial possibilities of the farthest reaches of the continent, produced dozens of maps, collected flora, fauna, and minerals, preserved a vast amount of scientific information in written records, and returned with all but one of the members of their remarkable expedition unharmed. The two intrepid leaders made tangible with stories, reports, and artifacts the significance of the continent Americans were about to possess. The nation would stretch "from sea to shining sea." At the same time, memorials imploring Jefferson to run for a third term began flooding the White House mailbox. State legislatures, in what was a demonstration of the Republican party's strength, passed resolutions hailing the president as the champion of the rights of man.

But the road ahead was full of bumps and potholes. During the summer of 1805, Jefferson was taking in the news that his erstwhile vice president was conspiring with the nation's highest-ranking army officer in the far West. Exploring a continent proved much easier than curbing an errant Burr. The president was also struggling to get Congress to appropriate money for his covert (and abortive) purchase of West Florida. Here his avidity for filling out American boundaries clashed with his stated principles about how to conduct public business. During these negotiations, he agreed on a bribe to the French, a secret fund, and even a contemplated alliance with Great Britain to secure his end. In one sense a familiar story of the political superego meeting the id of reality, Jefferson's second term brought him face to face with defeats that tamed his optimism.

Meanwhile the crisis over neutrality rights for American shippers inched toward a climax.

Hostilities between France and Great Britain—those persistent eighteenth-century enemies—had brought the United States prosperity. Despite Americans' aspirations for a continental future, their economy was still centered on the Atlantic. The French and British faced each other throughout the world: in India; along the west coast of Africa; in the Caribbean; and on the North American continent. Their far-flung colonies produced commodities and profits essential to their flourishing in peace and succeeding in war. As the neutral shippers for both belligerents, American merchants collected profits sizable enough to fund hundreds of other economic enterprises. Revenue from this expanding commerce enabled Jefferson to pay down the national debt and purchase Louisiana without financial strain. The carrying trade, as it was called, grew in the three years between 1803 and 1806. Intensified hostility between France and Britain interrupted this bonanza during the summer of 1805. Jefferson could not afford to ignore the situation; nor could he break his ingrained habit of moving first with idealistic intentions.

The model treaty that American diplomats had crafted at the moment of Independence now became a defense of American ships going wherever there was business. Principle and practicality blended when Americans talked about their trade. For them, economic and political liberty paired off naturally. Where men and their families enjoyed rights, they worked harder, and their hard work paid off in bigger harvests, yielding more grains and fibers to sell. So effortlessly did these causes and effects bond together that no American could think to disentangle them. Thomas Paine in *Common Sense* had bucked up Americans' courage to declare independence by reminding them that they would continue to prosper as long as "eating was the custom of Europe." The American economy did not depend upon frivolous artifices, but rather on the necessities of life—food crops for the stomach, fibers for clothing, wood products for shelter. One consequence of the American way of evaluating their economy was to overvalue its importance to Europe. Having hitched their national wagon to the star of universal progress, they went on to assume the self-evidence of a natural commercial order in which nations traded with each other on the basis of mutual benefit.

Jefferson's fight for neutral rights drew strength from this virtuous concept of commerce. His strong and strongly expressed moral sense exposed him to charges of hypocrisy. Unlike the Federalists, who accepted the world as a bad place in which one had to learn to maneuver skillfully, Jefferson bent to expediency but always sprang back to reassert principle.

While American voters were giving the champion of democracy a second term as president, Napoleon Bonaparte was taking on the trappings of royalty, having crowned himself emperor in a lavish ceremony at the Cathedral of Notre Dame in Paris. The new emperor's many enemies formed a coalition that spread war once again to most of Europe. France had a mighty army, brilliantly led by Napoleon. Great Britain, favored with a superb naval strategist in Lord Horatio Nelson, decisively gained control of the high seas after the battle of Trafalgar. Jefferson exclaimed, "What an awful spectacle does the world exhibit at this instant, one nation bestriding the continent of Europe like a Colossus, and another roaming unbridled on the ocean."[3] Whatever tolerance the warring giants of Europe had shown toward America's claim to freedom of the seas came to an end in 1806; the last years of Jefferson's presidency were much troubled by the belligerents' resolve to give each other no quarter.

Both countries relied on their overseas possessions for wealth. In May 1806, Britain announced that it was blockading the entire western coast of the European continent. In normal times, French shippers carried products from France's colonies to home ports. Faced with the likelihood that the superior British navy would devastate their merchant fleet, France turned to shippers in the United States in hopes that their neutrality would enable their safe passage through hostile waters. For America, these new developments meant being the pawn in yet another titanic struggle between France and Britain.

Britain held two bludgeons over American heads: the threat of impressments, and the seizure of ships suspected of violating its Rule of 1756. Both weapons were wielded with arrogant, vengeful energy. The Rule of 1756 stated that trade not allowed in time of peace would not be honored in time of war; that is, the British gave themselves the right to interfere with the shipping of neutral countries like the United States if they started visiting ports closed to them in peacetime. British naval vessels lay off the coast of the United States, ready to confiscate the cargoes of any ships suspected of carrying French goods. Being his party's leader as well as his nation's president, Jefferson defended the carrying trade because it was important to Northern Republicans. It probably added spice to the mix that Britain was the country being defied.

Impressment was the legal term applied to the Royal Navy's power to coerce British seamen to serve in time of war. Because shipping out with an American commercial vessel was much more attractive than naval service, British seamen frequently signed on as crew members of American ships. American skippers, pressed for hands, often asked deserters no questions; nor was it illegal for them to hire foreign seamen. As a result, British naval vessels regularly stopped American ships to search them for deserters. While Jefferson and his cabinet worried about the ease with which British deserters found berths on American ships, they reasoned that, in the absence of a commercial treaty with Great Britain, they were under no obligation to stop the practice. At one point, Jefferson did seek to avoid confrontations with the Royal Navy. He contemplated returning all known British subjects serving on American ships, only to discover that of the 18,000 able-bodied seamen engaged in American foreign trade almost half were subjects of George III!

In the midst of these crises, Jefferson's foreign policy attracted domestic critics. Alas for the president, the most vociferous came from within his own party. Success was the problem. As they won ever larger majorities in successive state and national elections, Republicans broke into factions. The eccentric and indomitable John Randolph took over the role Jefferson had played in the 1790s, scrutinizing every administrative act for evidence of moral failure. There is something delicious in his high-minded censure of Jefferson for employing secrecy, duplicity, and financial shenanigans to get the Spanish to part with the Floridas, or for vexing Britain when it was struggling against autocratic Napoleon. "I do not understand this double set of opinions and principles—the one ostensible, the other real," Randolph told Gallatin, adding a very Jeffersonian line: "I hold true wisdom and cunning to be utterly incompatible."[4]

Nothing came of the effort to bribe France to pressure Spain into selling the Floridas, but Randolph's criticism hardened into confirmed opposition. Joining him from time to time were the Pennsylvania Republicans, who arrayed themselves between the poles of the fiery democratic radicals and those moderates so conventional they could pass for Federalists. Jefferson had stirred the hopes of the radically egalitarian Republicans grouped around William Duane, the ardent editor of Philadelphia's *Aurora*. Those who espoused "the principles of '98"—articulated in opposition to the detested Sedition Act—wanted all civil offices swept of Federalists, the judiciary reformed, the powers of the Senate reduced, and the president's treaty-making powers restricted. For these men—mostly Virginians—a new term entered the political lexicon: Tertium Quid, "third thing," shortened simply to Quids.

Randolph's course of action exemplifies the classic contrast between those in and out of power, between opposing those with responsibility and exercising that responsibility. The situation did not lack poetic justice, for the Republicans had publicly repudiated Federalist tactics that smacked of putting national interest above principle, as Jefferson now found himself doing. The defection of Randolph, who had been Jefferson's leader in the House through the first administration, must have elated Federalists, though in fact Randolph's tendency to tilt at windmills, large and small, blunted his effectiveness. He signaled his break with the administration in an impassioned speech on the floor of Congress, followed by publication of a series of critical "letters," which added to the pressure Jefferson felt to dissuade his son-in-law from engaging in a duel with Randolph. Well might the president tell his correspondents that he could hardly bear the thought of two more years in office. And the worst was yet to come.

At a more practical level, Republican purists—Southern almost to a man—complained that the carrying trade did nothing to ferret out new markets for American farmers. The trade that burgeoned with Haiti in the wake of the rebellion was particularly vulnerable to congressional disapproval and was finally restricted. Nothing quite as explicitly revealed the country's commercial future as this expansion in the "neutral carrier" trade, which had no connection with American crops or products. To profit from running French goods through the British blockade demeaned the United States, according to Randolph, who concluded that "there is something ungenerous in taking advantage of a period when Great Britain is struggling for her very existence." One need not have been an Anglophilic Federalist to root for freedom-loving Englishmen pitted against the Johnny-come-lately French emperor.

The warfare between France and England had other ideological overtones. In 1793, enthusiasm for the French Revolution had stoked the radical zeal that led to the formation of the Republican opposition and ended in dislodging the Federalists. In the years since, France and England had become symbols for Americans, crystallizing the differences between those who sought orderly change under the law, with respect for status and tradition, and those who embraced the French Revolution's call for liberty, equality, fraternity. What might have provided simply a shorthand for political differences turned tricky when Federalists and Republicans pursued different foreign policy goals, the former aligning the nation with its former imperial sovereign, the latter seeking to break free of Britain's cultural and commercial influence. Both Federalists and Republicans had difficulty detaching themselves from the domestic significance of being an Anglophile or Galloman, even though the international scene was changing dramatically with every twist in the European war. The original attachments endured long after the issues moved from the political realm to the economic.

Fully aware of the importance of peace, Jefferson wanted to punish the British for their arrogant seizures of American ships on the high seas. Memorials from shippers and insurers began to pour into Washington. American merchants were up in arms because the British captures of their boats had driven the cost of insurance sky high. In early 1806, the president presented these memorials to Congress along with a recommendation to pass a mild Non-Importation Act designed to avoid occasions for confrontations with the British. A first step had been taken toward legislating a solution to the American situation.

The new year, 1807, opened with the news that Napoleon had responded to the British blockade with the Berlin Decrees, declaring a blockade of the British Isles. Next came new British orders in council, forbidding all shippers, neutral or otherwise, from engaging in the coastal trade between French ports in the Caribbean. On June 22, threats and bullying turned violent when the fifty-gun warship H.M.S. *Leopard* stopped the *Chesapeake*, a U.S. frigate, bound for the Mediterranean. The incident took place off the coast of Norfolk, Virginia, where a British squadron was lying in wait for French ships. The British wanted to search the *Chesapeake* for a cluster of deserters who had disappeared into Norfolk several months earlier. Refused permission to board, the British fired on the *Chesapeake*, killing three seamen and wounding eighteen others. The British then boarded the *Chesapeake* and plucked from the ship four men whom they believed to be deserters from the Royal Navy.

Arguably an act of war, the attack by the *Leopard* infuriated Jefferson. He summoned his cabinet to Washington. Citizens of Norfolk and nearby Portsmouth refused to provision any other British ships. Americans learned of the *Chesapeake* affair under alarming headlines like "British Outrage." But the Constitution was quite clear as to which branch of government could declare war, and

Congress would not meet for four more months. Jefferson issued a proclamation laying out the case for neutral rights and announcing the withdrawal of the hospitality of American waters and ports to the British Navy; then he bided his time.

In October, he delivered his seventh annual message to Congress, a scathing recapitulation of America's unhappy relations with Great Britain. His navy secretary, Robert Smith, called it "a manifesto against the British government." Jefferson himself preferred to think in terms of redressing injuries "old and new." Fifteen years earlier, as secretary of state, he had stunned the British minister to the United States with a 250-page refutation of the British compilation of American violations of the 1783 peace treaty. At that time Jefferson was battling against the pro-English measures of Treasury Secretary Hamilton, who secretly undercut him by telling the British emissary that Jefferson did not speak for the administration. In 1807 Hamilton was dead and Jefferson, very much alive and in possession of a good memory, gave vent to his fury at British arrogance, not to mention his frustration with the power that undergirded that arrogance. In some ways echoing the Declaration of Independence, which had also detailed American grievances against Great Britain, the seventh annual message folded outrage over the *Chesapeake* affair into the history of Anglo-American relations since the 1760s.[5]

While the president, his cabinet, and Congress waited to see how Great Britain would respond to their formal protests, France and England bore down harder on American shippers, France becoming as zealous in closing continental ports to neutral ships as the English had been to do so elsewhere around the globe. The number of confiscated cargoes mounted; searches of American ships for deserters increased. Estimates of the losses to the French in 1807 were put at $10 million, with British confiscations many times larger. Because of the difficulties his administration had enforcing the limited Non-Importation Act, Jefferson moved toward measures that would cut off all trade between the United States and the European belligerents. An embargo would keep Americans and their goods out of harm's way; it would minimize the risk of war; and it would hit the British in their pocketbooks—or at least the pocketbooks of those powerful Englishmen whose wealth depended on exports to the United States.

On December 18, the president asked Congress for a complete ban on all international shipping, and for authority to build up the military. The Senate acted quickly on the president's request, and a week later the House followed suit. To a friend, Jefferson explained that the "embargo keeping at home our vessels, cargoes & seamen, saves us the necessity of making their capture the cause of immediate war: for if going to England, France had determined to take them; if to any other place, England was to take them. Till they return to some sense of moral duty therefore, we keep within ourselves."[6] With his usual optimism, Jefferson expected spring to bring a resolution to the conflict, with France and Great Britain recognizing America's rights as a neutral country. How very badly his optimism misled him.

The promptness of Congress's response was no measure of the law's popularity. In fact, merchants in the Northern cities were already restive under the first, very mild nonimportation law. Federalists spread the argument that, while appearing impartial, the embargo in fact singled out England. A floor battle over the embargo actually led to the first duel between congressmen. When a Tennessee Republican rose to denounce the "petty scribblers" who circulated reports of a French influence behind the president's policy, a New York Federalist delivered a harangue evoking an unseen hand, surrounded by "darkness, secrecy and impenetrable mystery." To this, the Tennessean retorted that the speaker must himself be "the screen to convey these groundless slanders to the public—the common trumpeter who gives no importance to what he makes public." When mutual demands for a retraction went unanswered, the two transferred their rancor to the dueling grounds.[7]

Meanwhile, merchants more pragmatically took on the task of evading the embargo as part and parcel of engaging in a hazardous business. Enforcement became a nightmare, and a long one, as the sanguine hopes for a speedy capitulation from Britain or France faded. Tormented by contradictory demons—Would he flinch in the embargo's execution? Would he plunge the nation into war if keeping American ships at home failed? Would coercion do more evil than good?—Jefferson stayed the course: he enforced the embargo while enduring month after month of personal vilification, opposition furor, and on-the-ground fraud. Convinced that the only alternative to war was the embargo, Jefferson allowed it to threaten every political principle he held dear.

By the time Americans were ready to elect a new president, in the fall of 1808, the embargo had dragged on for a year, with terrible losses to American shippers and to the farmers, artisans, and shipwrights who counted on them to transport or use their products. The embargo nearly split the famously consensual Jefferson cabinet. Unwilling to abandon it in December, Jefferson found a new tactic: let the incoming president, James Madison, decide what to do. After all Madison had been intimately engaged in the diplomacy of the United States as Jefferson's secretary of state since 1801. For the next three months, Jefferson ceded leadership to him and to Treasury Secretary Albert Gallatin, who was slated to be the next secretary of state. As 1808 turned into 1809, Jefferson's attention became riveted to home. He canceled newspaper subscriptions and began sending his furniture, wine, and books back to Monticello.

The congressional elections registered the unpopularity of Jefferson's embargo. The Republicans kept their Senate seats, but lost twenty-four seats in the House of Representatives to end up with a 94–48 majority, a figure that still points to their remarkable dominance. Outrage at the embargo and the government that was enforcing it was concentrated in the Northeast—especially Massachusetts—where talk of secession was backed by huge demonstrations. Coastal towns denounced the president in fiery resolutions. Newspapers rallied opponents with such exhortations as this: "Nerve your arms with vengeance against the despot who would wrest the inestimable germ of independence from you, and you shall be conquerors. Give ear no longer to the siren voice of democracy and Jeffersonian liberty."[8]

The nadir of Jefferson's presidency, these months saw New Englanders threatening open resistance to the law while Congress, balanced fairly evenly between antiwar and antiembargo blocs, dithered. In January it passed the Enforcing Act, which made more onerous and extensive the embargo's coercive machinery, but the game was over. By that date there were but two alternatives to repeal: war, or continuation of a measure that threatened the union. A month later Congress, bereft of direction from Jefferson, voted to repeal the embargo. The repeal was to take effect on March 4, when there would be a new president. American shippers could now take their chances on the waters of the Atlantic.

In the months that followed, Madison faced much the same situation that dogged Jefferson's last years in office, and with the same puny arrows in his quiver. French and British harassment of American shippers continued until Great Britain defeated Napoleon at Waterloo and, weary of war, composed its differences with the United States.

Unwilling to face the failure of his policy, Jefferson lamented that Congress had retreated from the principled stand of the embargo only to face a kind of lottery, ruining many while paying bonanza profits to those merchants who came away unscathed in the perilous trade. For a president who hated both speculation and discord, it was a sorry conclusion to his public career.

The precipitous decline in Jefferson's popularity had its humorous side. In a bizarre case that came before the Philadelphia County Court of Common Pleas, two booksellers had agreed to exchange, even-steven, engravings of Jefferson and Washington, each having a backlog of one set. As Jefferson's second term wore on, the bookseller who had to exchange his Washingtons for engravings of Jefferson balked and was taken to court for failing to carry out his agreement. He defended himself by pointing out that Jefferson's popularity "was sinking so rapidly that his likenesses (which of course were depreciated with the original) had already fallen to almost nothing." He further argued that "as there was no chance of HIS ever being re-elected, there was no probability of THEIR ever rising." The court, no doubt inspired by Chief Justice Marshall's rulings, upheld the contract.[9]

The embargo had ignited all the crossed wires of Jefferson's foreign policy. It vigorously assailed British authority on the high seas. It avenged American seamen for impressment, an ill that went back to the colonial era. It made a powerful statement about the seriousness with which Americans took the principle of freedom of the seas as set forth in their model treaty. It put teeth into the "no entangling alliances" position. It reflected Jefferson's willingness to make extreme concessions to avoid war. Unfortunately, none of these factors could make it work. Neither the British nor the French yielded; meanwhile, American commerce withered away. The willingness of the United States to withdraw from international trade rather than be preyed upon by warring European powers counted for naught. Only the extraordinary popularity of the Republican party permitted Jefferson's perseverance, and finally even Republican congressmen bolted. During the agonizing months of enforcement, Jefferson's position became more doctrinaire. Increasingly he saw the forces of good struggling for ascendancy against evil. Morality lost, in his view, when the embargo failed. Its defeat gave stark proof that might made right.

The fifteen-month ordeal of the embargo must have confused most people. Despite the risks of capture and confiscations, merchants and shippers had profited enormously from the lucrative carrying trade, their profits bringing prosperity to the rest of the country. While some people benefited from start-up manufacturing ventures (the embargo, after all, provided total protection), renewed trade in 1809 wiped out most of these enterprises. Politically, the embargo heightened awareness of how Southern and Northern interests differed. Southern Republicans proved the most hostile to the carrying trade. Northern Republicans differed from Northern Federalists in their appreciation of free trade, government restraint, and a widened ambit of opportunity, all qualities battered by the embargo and its vigorous enforcement. The aggression of the Royal Navy rekindled antipathy to Great Britain, but without nurturing pro-French sentiments. Despite the importance of foreign commerce, Americans were being readied for a long century of isolation from international concerns. Jefferson's West beckoned, more appealing than ever.

Before he left office, Jefferson had an opportunity to strike a blow against the hideous international slave trade. The Constitution had specifically protected the trade with an awkwardly worded provision: "the importation of such persons as the states shall think proper to admit shall not be prohibited prior to 1808." The stipulation barred any congressional ban on the trade for twenty years. After that, passage of a ban would be constitutionally permissible.

At the earliest possible moment, Jefferson placed before Congress legislation that would end American participation in this cruelest of all commercial undertakings. Despite the conspicuous flaws in his diplomacy, Jefferson's foreign policy in this one act did more to extend the realm of freedom than any deed of his contemporaries in the age of democratic revolutions.

Coming to Terms with Thomas Jefferson

Americans' most pressing history assignment is coming to terms with Thomas Jefferson. His greatness as a revolutionary leader and a president is imprinted across the land. His stirring rhetoric finds its way into hundreds of speeches and books every year. Yet the contradiction between the Declaration of Independence's evocation of "the right to life, liberty and the pursuit of happiness" and its author's status as a slaveholder troubles us more than ever before. John Kennedy thrilled the public when he told the Nobel laureates assembled in the White House dining room that they were the most extraordinary collection of talents that had ever been gathered there "with the possible exception of when Thomas Jefferson dined alone." The line would not play as well today. No one doubts that Jefferson gave unstintingly of those talents. The difficulty lies elsewhere. Jefferson failed to disentangle himself from the crimes of slavery, and thus made it harder for us to cope with its bitter legacy.

Jefferson's reputation has plummeted twice before: during the Civil War, when Northerners blamed states' rights doctrines for promoting secession; and at the end of the nineteenth century, when unrest among farmers and workers made Jefferson's democratic rhetoric sound dangerous.[1] The first charge is anachronistic, but he richly deserves blame for convincing ordinary Americans that they should exercise their power. Jefferson's states'-rights views were always in tension with his powerful nation-building tendencies, and he saw state power as offering a balance to federal power, not a platform for separation. The North's victory in the Civil War rendered the issue moot. Not so popular rule. The upper-class leaders who ran the country after the war devalued Jefferson for his faith in the people. When America's farmers turned into defiant populists, they feared the participatory politics he had championed. Even the Progressives found Jefferson's strict construction of the Constitution and his laissez-faire economic policies disabling when they sought to curb the power of the new industrialists. Reformers then confronted problems that required affirmative effective government, not the negative government Jefferson had favored. Jefferson had to step aside in the American pantheon for state-builders like Alexander Hamilton.

Nothing quite captures the disesteem accorded Jefferson in the closing decade of the nineteenth century as well as the apology in Paul Leicester Ford's introduction to his edition of Jefferson's papers. Explaining to readers that Jefferson had been charged with "contradictions and instability," with "hypocrisy, opportunism, and even lack of any political principles," Ford held democracy up to contempt. "Unlike the Federalists," he explained, "Jefferson was willing to discard the tradition of ages—that the people must be protected against themselves by the brains, money and 'better elements' of the country—and for this reason American democracy made him its chosen agent and mouth-piece." Ford found Jefferson's character and conduct filled with serious flaws, but he discerned that the people in some subtle way had understood him. They realized, he said, that Jefferson's controlling aim was neither national independence nor state sovereignty but rather to secure for Americans "the ever enduring privilege of personal freedom." Not quite as dismissive as Ford, Brooks and Henry Adams also penned critical estimates of the rival of their great-grandfather John Adams, but not without anxiety. Henry returned a manuscript that Brooks had sent him with the exasperated note, "For God Almighty's sake, leave Jefferson alone!"[2]

But it's hard to leave Jefferson alone. His ideas are implicated in too many currents of our national life, past and present. The character of our democracy remains unsettled and begs for analysis. Jefferson's simultaneous endorsement of human equality and racial inequality allowed generations of Americans to claim democratic virtues while ignoring civil rights abuses that undermined those virtues. His particular take on freedom as the realm of free choice and voluntary action has fostered a powerful antigovernment tradition in the United States. Ideas about limiting the power of government that developed in an era marked by paternalistic intrusiveness, such as the eighteenth century, play differently at a time when private corporations wield vast informal power that needs checking. Woodrow Wilson made that point in *The New Freedom*:

> I feel confident that if Jefferson were living in our day he would see what we see. . . . Without the watchful interference, the resolute interference of the government, there can be no fair play between individuals and such powerful institutions as the trust.

The universal affirmations in the Declaration of Independence also run athwart today's appreciation of cultural diversity. If what is protected are the commonalities we share, how should the law respond to our differences?

Against these deficits are two of Jefferson's achievements of rare worth: the championing of participatory politics and the memorable expression of what freedom means and who its enemies are. Jefferson built a modern political party and forced his establishmentarian opponents to copy him. Two-party politics have been with us, for better or worse, ever since. Jefferson's fight against bigotry rallied advocates for religious freedom—not mere toleration—after the Revolution. His "wall of separation" offers a rare demonstration of the power of words, just three of them.

In many ways the enemies of freedom that Jefferson railed

against were paper tigers: quasi-aristocrats, verbose clerics, aging traditionalists. American colonial experience had already produced a unique social order all set to make manifest its latent values. This helps explain why a man whose greatest gift was inspiring others with his rhetoric could topple the Federalist elite so handily. While for many years in tune with the public, Jefferson's reputation has changed as Americans' political attention has gravitated around issues of race, government power, informal tyrannies, the extension of democratic rights, and freedom's flashy expression. Jefferson's reputation has waxed and waned with the salience of these concerns. Not surprisingly, it rebounded with the New Deal.

Back in power after a long Republican era, the Democrats claimed Jefferson as their party founder and prepared for the bicentennial of his birth in 1943. The symbolic play of favorite Founding Fathers had its humorous side. Interested in honoring theirs, the Democratic Congress tied the wish to the need for increasing postal revenue. They voted to raise the price of first-class mail to three cents, putting Jefferson on the new three-cent stamp and leaving George Washington undisturbed on the old one-cent stamp. Bringing an end to a long period of neglect, Congress also created the Thomas Jefferson Memorial Commission to site, design, and construct a monument in the nation's capital. Franklin Roosevelt, another member of an elite who championed "the little man," officiated at the ceremonial groundbreaking in 1938, the memorial itself being dedicated on April 13, 1943, with a plaster statue of Jefferson. (Metal had gone to war.)

Out of the Thomas Jefferson Memorial Commission came the most ambitious publishing venture in American history: a complete edition of Jefferson's papers. Since he saved the letters he received and copied ones he wrote with a machine, the body of papers totals some 35,000 items—personal and official letters, legislative reports, addresses, and executive orders. Princeton University Press brought out the first volume in 1950. More than a half-century and twenty-nine volumes later, and with a parallel series now started to cover his retirement years, the entire edition may be completed by the tricentennial of Jefferson's birth in 2043 or, failing that, by the time of the centennial of the publishing project itself, in 2050.

From this pinnacle of respect in the 1940s, Jefferson's reputation has slowly descended. The civil rights movement that began with school integration and voting access in the 1960s and continues today with affirmative action and reparations debates roused historians to examine Jefferson's record on slavery. As the owner of more than two hundred men, women, and children Jefferson lived in a slave milieu, so it is probably not surprising that closer inspection revealed ambivalences and evasions. Jefferson repeatedly denounced the institution, but he never found the courage to extricate himself or his fellow Virginians from its toils. He penned some of the most powerful lines exposing the evils of slavery, but backed away from attacking the institution as his power to do something about it increased.

It has been said that the Founding Fathers attacked slavery where it was weakest and left it alone where it was strongest. Jefferson fits this picture very well. He tried to get a denunciation of the slave trade into the Declaration of Independence. He called slavery a "moral and political depravity." He regularly condemned it in personal letters. He even proposed that all new territories be closed to slavery, a measure that lost by one vote in the Continental Congress. This effort of Jefferson's undoubtedly prepared the way for the Northwest Ordinance, which did keep slavery out of Ohio, Michigan, Wisconsin, Illinois, and Minnesota while they were territories. He contemplated a revision of the Virginia constitution that would provide for gradual emancipation—but he insisted that the freed slaves could not remain in the state. This was the dilemma that Jefferson created for himself.

To justify his resistance to a biracial society of free blacks and whites, Jefferson laid bare the psychological dynamics of the master-slave relations with images as vivid as a poet's:

The whole commerce between master and slave is a perpetual exercise of the most boisterous passions, the unremitting despotism on the one part, and degrading submissions on the other. Our children see this, and learn to imitate it; for man is an imitative animal. . . . The parent storms, the child looks on, catches the lineaments of wrath, puts on the same airs in the circle of smaller slaves, gives loose to his worst of passions, and thus nursed, educated, and daily exercised in tyranny, cannot but be stamped by it with odious peculiarities.[3]

It was slavery itself, in Jefferson's opinion, that made necessary the separation of the races after emancipation. Former master and former slave had to avoid the effects of "deep rooted prejudices entertained by the whites; ten thousand recollections, by the blacks, of the injuries they have sustained." Posing the problem this way made it unsolvable, and the conclusion was unjust, since it would be the freed slaves who had to move. A simple calculation would have demonstrated the impracticality of relocating a fifth of the nation's population. Yet the American Colonization Society, which proposed just that, continued to attract members for decades, including a young Abraham Lincoln.

Slavery was very much on Jefferson's mind when he entered the presidency. While slavery had always been viewed as a deplorable condition, the institution itself had been accepted among the necessary evils of life, like dying. Then, with remarkable suddenness, abolition became a topic stirring intense agitation during the closing decades of the eighteenth century. All the Northern states had begun to put an end to the repugnant institution, most of them through laws compelling emancipation gradually according to age. Not only had these states furnished a model for extinguishing the legality of human property, they had made good on the ringing affirmations of equal rights in the Declaration of Independence. Jefferson never referred in writing to these momentous acts, though they undoubtedly prompted him to write a friend that "the hour of emancipation is advancing." He might have recommended that Louisiana enter the Union with a gradual emancipation statute like that of Pennsylvania or New York. He could have, had he not been more concerned with the aftermath of black freedom. Recoiling from the violence of the Haitian revolution, he urged white Southerners to figure out where the "colored emigrants" of the future might go, adding grimly: "[I]f something is not done, and soon done, we shall be the murderers of our own children."[4]

During his presidency, Jefferson asked Rufus King, then American minister to Great Britain, to seek permission to send "slaves guilty of insurgency" to the British colony of Sierra Leone. Here he was reacting to the execution of the participants in the aborted Gabriel Prosser revolt of 1800. But little more was heard from him about emancipation, and in his later years he ceased to criticize slavery publicly. He justified his unwillingness by saying that words could not achieve the end desired and that candor would diminish the "confidence and good will" of a large group of people—presumably, other slaveholders—thereby lessening his power to do other kinds of good things.[5] His shepherding through Congress a ban on the African slave trade in 1808 was his last public act against slavery.

There was pleading from ardent admirers such as his young neighbor Edward Coles, who brought his slaves to Illinois and freed them there. Jefferson wrote Coles that he rejoiced that "the flame of liberty" was being kindled in the breasts of the younger generation, yet he would not go beyond such platitudes. In fact, he spent the last half of his letter cautioning Coles about the negative consequences of "amalgamation" and the likelihood that freed adult blacks would become "pests in society."[6] "A strange uniform—the skin," the French philosophe Pierre-Samuel Du Pont once remarked in a letter to Jefferson. Jefferson did not reply to this poignant metaphor, perhaps because his prejudice had never been just skin deep.

Jefferson shared this moral flaw with other great revolutionary figures. George Washington, James Madison, and John Marshall are all iconic figures in American history, and all were slaveholders. Over half the signers of the Declaration of Independence held slaves. Washington, to his great credit, freed his, but only in his will. Madison, the so-called father of the Constitution, did not speak out on the subject, and Marshall, the Constitution's most famous interpreter, strove to keep discussion of slavery out of the court. He privately rebuked those who sought to address the contradiction of freedom-loving Americans assiduously protecting their slave property.

Not having raised our expectations with affirmations of natural rights, these leaders have not disappointed us. Jefferson's buying, selling, and owning of men and women has disturbed the pages of our history as no other's has. But there's more to this complex situation. Jefferson also made the expansion of human liberty a realistic national goal. In that sense, he has elevated us and let us down at the same time. We want Founding Fathers who summon us to a civic calling higher than going to the polls and paying taxes. Jefferson did that; his words soar above the banalities of daily life, acting as both inspiration and goad. That Jefferson carries the odium of slavery for his generation is a wry tribute to his status as the voice for America's better self.

Few people—certainly no other leaders of the American Revolution—have written so forthrightly about slavery and the race relations it fathered. One can search the papers of Washington, Monroe, Marshall, Madison, and John Randolph and never find anything faintly similar in introspective honesty. Nor did Jefferson flinch from the conundrums of slavery that tormented him. He said forthrightly that in Virginia, from where he had made his observations about the slaves' debased condition, "the opportunities for the developing of their genius were not favorable." He also expressed pleasure at the "hopeful advances" Africans were making in the early nineteenth century "towards their reestablishment on an equal footing with the other colors of the human family."

Jefferson recognized that his suspicions about blacks' intelligence were also irrelevant, for humanity, not intelligence, laid the basis for rights and respect. Although Isaac Newton was "superior to others in understanding," he said, Newton "was not therefore lord of the person or property of others."[7] What Jefferson couldn't do was think himself and his country into a solution to the problem as he posed it: the ending of an institution so pernicious that it had permanently poisoned the souls of its perpetrators and victims.

Nor did Jefferson obscure his race prejudices. He constructed a series of comparisons in his *Notes* to prove that the Africans' "inferiority is not the effect merely of their condition of life." In this, his one book, he examined in great detail the physical and social differences between whites, Native Americans, and blacks, raising the purely gratuitous, rhetorical question of whether the "fine mixtures of red and white" were not "preferable to that external monotony . . . that immoveable veil of black." Concluding his examination, Jefferson advanced it "as a suspicion only, that the blacks . . . are inferior to the whites in the endowments both of body and mind." Although this line is frequently quoted as a reproach to Jefferson, rarely cited is his acknowledgment that the opinion "must be hazarded with great diffidence."[8] For the rest of his life, people sent him evidence of the achievements of African Americans, to which he would invariably respond with expressions of approval and reminders that his had been only a "suspicion."

For Americans, the nadir of their esteem for Jefferson came in 1998, with reports that DNA tests had determined that a male in Jefferson's family fathered Sally Hemings's last child, Eston. No longer was it possible to protect him from the old charge that he conceived children with his slave and reared his own kin in bondage. Well might Jefferson write, "I tremble for my country when I consider that God is just: that his justice cannot sleep forever."[9] He followed this oft-quoted remark with speculations of a much grimmer nature—the possibility that "a revolution of the wheel of fortune" might lead to "an exchange of situations" between slaves and their masters. Jefferson was no atheist, but he rarely invoked a personal God who would intervene in human affairs—except when he talked about God's judgment of slavery. Then he recalled the God of the Old Testament, full of wrath against injustice. Jefferson knew that he lived and benefited from a system drenched in sin.

Although they are rarely asked together, questions about slavery can be fruitfully linked to another puzzle about Jefferson: Why did a member of America's wealthiest, most cosseted elite make it his life's work to change the lot of poor white farmers and laborers—the common people of the country? Jefferson's ardor for eliminating the hierarchies of status to make way for a society of white male equals never flagged. He clearly identified with ordinary white men as he could not do with enslaved men or even Native Americans. Toussaint-Louverture and Tecumseh were remarkable contemporaries with whom he had to deal as president. Each fought to preserve self-determination for his people, but Jefferson seemed indifferent to their greatness. More important, he resisted folding their people into that grand design for progress that sustained his zeal for political action. He did not doubt that God had given them the same rights as other men, but he did doubt that they would know how to use freedom. An attempt to understand this want of sympathy and imagination in one of history's most intuitive politicians leads directly to the content of Jefferson's hopes for a new order for mankind.

Jefferson's freedom was for adult white men who could fend for themselves because of certain inherent qualities—rationality, the drive for self-improvement, the capacity to work independently and to cooperate without coercion. The assertion that all men are alike in their aspirations to freedom as well as their capacity to pursue independent lives provided the scientific underpinning for his creed. If other men did not respond in an individually responsible manner, as did the Europeans' descendants in the United States, then it must be nature that had excluded them from participation in the great era of freedom opening up, as nature surely had excluded women. The presumed universality (among Europeans) of these human traits gave Americans confidence in a future in which retrograde monarchies would finally turn to republican forms of governance. Jefferson made this explicit when he told Joseph Priestley, "It is impossible not to be sensible that we are acting for all mankind;

that circumstances denied to others, but indulged to us, have imposed on us the duty of proving what is the degree of freedom and self-government in which a society may venture to leave its individual members."[10]

Jefferson held on to his one grand project: to reconstruct government so that the ordinary men of his race might live by the light of their own wisdom, unmolested by upper-class folly, supercilious theories about lower-class inferiority, or authoritarian laws to tell them what was good for them. We tend to see his selective attention as inconsistent, contradictory, even hypocritical, but the paradox is so blatant, there is probably another answer. Unquestionably, Jefferson believed in the *rights* of all men—but he found evidence of the capacity for personal autonomy only in white men. The frustration of their scope of action by oppressive institutions roused him to action, while the abuse of the slaves' humanity filled him with despair. It is somewhat ironic, but also revealing, that the improvidence and lack of discipline that Jefferson attributed to slaves, the Federalists found in ordinary white men as well.

In some of Jefferson's most powerful statements, a strain of anger at economic exploitation surfaces that unwittingly calls to mind slavery, as when he excoriated defenders of privilege:

> Still further to constrain the brute force of the people, they deem it necessary to keep them down by hard labor, poverty and ignorance, and to take from them, as from bees, so much of their earnings, as that unremitting labor shall be necessary to obtain a sufficient surplus barely to sustain a scanty and miserable life.

The only explanation for this anomaly is that he evidently believed that slaves were "better fed, warmer clothed, and labor less than the journeymen or day-laborers of England." Jefferson hastened to correct the impression that he was "justifying the wrong we have committed on a foreign people, by the example of another nation committing equal wrongs on their own subjects," adding: "on the contrary, there is nothing I would not sacrifice to a practicable plan of abolishing every vestige of this moral and political depravity." Still, the comparison is strange for a man who prized freedom above all else.[11]

Jefferson's starting premise encouraged a critical attitude toward difference. Women were naturally different; blacks were naturally different; Native Americans suffered from an attachment to a backward way of life. Jefferson clearly enjoyed the company of women, and he adored his daughters. He prescribed a rigorous regimen for them and sent hectoring letters inquiring about their progress studying French and playing the piano. He took their development seriously. He treated them very much as rational creatures, with the reasoning capacity that in men justified personal autonomy.

What is striking about Jefferson's attitude toward women as a sex is how unreflective he was about the meaning of their existence. For a man who tolerated few unexamined assumptions, he slipped easily into the facile conviction that women were created for men's pleasure. Adding insult to injury, he insisted that few things were less pleasurable to men than women busying themselves with politics. He could be quite patronizing on this subject, as when he wrote Anne Willing Bingham that "our good ladies" "have been too wise to wrinkle their foreheads with politics." Instead "they are contended to soothe and calm the minds of their husbands returning ruffled from political debate." He tormented himself over the legacy of slavery and the possibility of inherent racial differences, but never addressed the evident competence of the women around him and what implications it might have for their civil rights. This is the attitude that prompted him to rebuff Gallatin, when the latter suggested naming women to some of the minor federal offices. One can only hope that future assessments of Jefferson will confront his views of women with a seriousness that eluded him.

The equality Jefferson espoused was political equality and equality of respect among white men. He, like others, recommended legislation that would disperse legacies to avoid concentrations of wealth. "I am conscious that an equal division of property is impracticable," he wrote Madison, "but the consequences of this enormous inequality producing so much misery to the bulk of mankind, legislators cannot invent too many devices for subdividing property, only taking care to let their subdivisions go hand in hand with the natural affections of the human mind." It was attention to this latter element that led him to reject explicitly the arbitrary spreading of wealth, as when he wrote: "To take from one, because it is thought that his own industry and that of his fathers has acquired too much, in order to spare to others, who, or whose fathers have not exercised equal industry and skill, is to violate arbitrarily the first principle of association, the guarantee to every one of a free exercise of his industry, and the fruits acquired by it." In this classic—for him— way of wedding the normative to the natural, Jefferson fused the popular power of the people, democracy, to the individual freedom and limited government that fired his reform engines. As he wrote his old friend Benjamin Rush, "I have sworn upon the altar of God, eternal hostility against every form of tyranny over the mind of man."[12]

Such rhetorical flourishes have got Jefferson in trouble recently, particularly one line that he wrote soon after he left France in 1789. It came in a response to a letter from his former secretary, William Short, who had become concerned about the violent turn of the French Revolution. Jefferson replied with some hyperbole that "the liberty of the whole earth was depending on the issue of the contest." And to emphasize the point, he added, "[R]ather than it should have failed I would have seen the earth desolated; were there but an Adam and Eve left in every country, and left free, it would be better than as it now is."[13] This brings to mind his earlier sally that the tree of liberty must be refreshed from time to time by the blood of patriots and tyrants. Obviously Jefferson was not contemplating the desolation of the earth but rather flamboyantly emphasizing that the failure of the French Revolution would snuff out reform hopes everywhere. Those who hold otherwise probably wish to flay him for other reasons.

Regard for Jefferson has been brought low for more than slave-holding. His reputation has shared in the decline of political idealism. The very extravagance of Jefferson's affirmation of freedom has generated critics who, not unlike Federalists two centuries ago, fear the neglect of good order, common sense, and sensitivity to other social values. Equally suspect to them is the social engineering that Jefferson engaged in when he pursued policies that undermined the existing hierarchical authority of magistrates, ministers, legislators, and, inferentially, fathers. The true conservatives are those who view as dangerous the man or woman who resists the conventions, most of which have stood the critical test of time. Perhaps because America has so long figured as a blank canvas for visionary designs, it has abounded in both reformers and their critics, their ascendancy oscillating over time.

Another strain in American conservative thought sets idealism against practicality, with the insinuation that those filled with idealistic goals will be hopelessly incompetent in the field of action. High-mindedness hobbles efficiency, in this view. The very act of thinking of how the world might be made more just is sufficient proof of terminal dreaminess. The case of Jefferson, America's ur-reformer, defies this subtle ridicule of reformers. Not only was he a meticulous record keeper, but his capacity to set realistic priorities enabled him to delegate authority and keep an eye on all the significant issues that came through his executive offices. His willingness to work long hours ensured that he was always prepared to back up his position with detailed research, as when he presented the British minister with a 250-page examination of British claims against the United States, or wrote a learned treatise on riparian law for the litigation between Edward Livingston and the U.S. government over ownership of a prize piece of river real estate in New Orleans. More to the point of his effectiveness was Jefferson's perseverance. Even his least effective policy, the embargo, offers a kind of verification. He couldn't let go of the effort to compel the British and French to honor American rights on the high seas, even if those rights were still but a glow on the horizon of international politics.

Jefferson had in abundance what most people are lucky to have in small doses: imagination. As his presidency shows, his power as a leader came from mobilizing a latent democratic movement among ordinary voters while closing the door on the genteel leadership that the Federalists offered. Alexis de Tocqueville came to the United States in the 1830s to view Europe's future in the world's first egalitarian society. A full generation earlier, Jefferson had mounted the campaign that brought that society into existence. He fitted democratic mores into the country's new political framework, tongue and groove. The Federalists had hoped that the United States might become a purer version of Great Britain with deference to wealth, family, and learning to ease the transition to self-government. Jefferson would have none of this. Confident of ordinary men's ability to govern themselves, he swept elite assumptions out of government. A New York conservative described Jefferson as the best rubber-off of dust he had ever met. The metaphor is apt because it was Jefferson's peculiar attitude to the settled and stationary—those things that collect dust—that separated him from almost all of his peers.

So alien to Washington, Hamilton, Adams, Marshall, and a host of lesser Federalists was Jefferson's sponsorship of expressive, participatory politics that they could only ascribe his democratic enthusiasms to ignoble motives: to an appetite for popularity or a suspect condescension. No gentleman, surely, could rationalize the irreverence and rambunctiousness associated with Jeffersonian club meetings and demonstrations. Hamilton epitomized this distaste in his near-hysterical plea to John Jay "to prevent an *Atheist* in religion, and a *Fanatic* in politics, from getting possession of the helm of state." Young Federalists tarred Jefferson with the brush of the French radicalism that produced the Reign of Terror. They continued to refer to Republicans as "American Jacobins" long after the French Jacobins had gone to the guillotine. Nothing could induce them to construe popular participation as anything other than a defeat for good sense and ancient wisdom. "Had our people been what they were in '76," one wrote, "Jefferson would not have been president in 1801." "Were they now what they were in '89," he continued, "he could not be president in 1805. The people have changed."[14]

Interestingly, "the people" figured prominently in the thinking of both camps. Basic to Jefferson's advocacy of limited government was the conviction that white men were basically orderly and cooperative, their better natures long hidden by the oppression they had suffered under. The Federalists affirmed a fundamental human nature, but one less benign, as in Fisher Ames's evocation of "the natural vanity, presumption, and restlessness of the human heart."[15] Strong fathers, churches, and governments were needed precisely to ward off the corruption and anarchy these qualities promoted. So horrified were the Federalists at the thought of a democratic experiment that historians have treated many of their statements as evidence of hysteria rather than expressions of what were then common political convictions.

Underpinning antidemocratic convictions was the deeply ingrained sense of superiority possessed by those with refinement, learning, and wealth. In an age when few went to college and cultivated tastes were even scarcer, members of the elite assumed that they understood and appreciated ideas and objects beyond the ken of ordinary Americans. Jefferson perplexed people like Henry and Brooks Adams just because he was so erudite himself and yet he persisted in inflating the political capacities of the unlearned. Surely there must be deceit here, some pandering to the vulgar. How could he be so hostile to the social hierarchies that had created great learning, great art, great wisdom in the first place?

Jefferson's first critics had trouble understanding his indifference to what Europeans might think of American performances in self-government. His predecessors in the White House strove mightily to acquire the formality of European governments, as they worked to secure the allegiance of America's own elite. Federalists, especially, wanted to prove themselves in English eyes, to follow their forms and live up to their expectations. Jefferson strove to debunk their Anglophilia. When they failed to follow his lead, he became convinced that the Federalists wished to reintroduce "the rags of royalty" so recently cast off. Jefferson turned informality—even negligence in matters of decorum—into a political virtue and seemed to take pleasure in insulting those with social pretensions. Where they looked to tradition to provide guidance, he distrusted old ways. He even proposed that the American electorate vote on all its laws every nineteen years—what he calculated to be the length of a generation—to put into practice his famous affirmation that the earth belonged to the living. And he discovered many American voters who shared his views, in the middle class that was growing under the nurturing sunlight of prosperity.

In the waning years of Jefferson's life, opposition to slavery mounted. Reflecting on these years, Henry Adams insisted that slavery "drove the whole Puritan community back on its Puritanism."[16] What he didn't say was that it also reanimated the righteous spirit of the Elect—as Jefferson intuited when he became incensed by Northern efforts in 1819 to check the entrance into the Union of Missouri as a slave state. Having fought New England's Federalists for so long, Jefferson had difficulty ceding the moral advantage to those unreconstructed elitists. And New Englanders dubbed Jefferson's class a slavocracy. Gerrit Smith, a prominent New York reformer, summarized a widely shared view that regional differences were based on disparities in character between the people of the North and those of the South. What he didn't say was that Northerners imaginatively thought of their "nation" as the United States, leaving the South with its peculiar institution and a particular regional culture.

An aging Thomas Jefferson perceived this situation and began urging Virginia leaders to support local colleges and academies. Earlier, when his grandson Francis Eppes had been ready for college, he had sent him to Columbia, but now Jefferson concluded that Columbia, Harvard, Princeton, and Pennsylvania no longer served Southern students. Estimating that there must be "five hundred of our own sons, imbibing opinions and principles in discord with their own country," Jefferson declared that "the signs of the times admonish us to call them" back. "If knowledge is power, we should look to its advancement at home" rather than trust "to those who are against us in position and principle, to fashion to their own form the minds and affections of our youth," he repeated in a letter to John Taylor. The issue of slavery had decomposed the Union into sections. Even the man who had built the first national political party fell victim to the corruption.

Approaching eighty, Jefferson had ceased to be a good barometer of public trends. He minimized the moral force of the antislavery movement and exaggerated the threat of a Federalist resurgence. In 1800, his democratizing program had represented a dramatic rupture with both the style and the substance of American governance. By the time of his death, participatory politics stood at the core of American political culture. Yet nothing is so hard to detect in the past as those novelties that have subsequently become familiar. So completely did Jeffersonian ideals triumph that it is hard for us to take seriously an opposition to them that propagated the view that the people, lacking good judgment, needed an upper class to direct the nation's affairs. To say, for instance, that Jefferson mobilized his contemporaries to strike down privilege and extend the ambit of free choice seems too ordinary an effort to warrant comment. To say, further, that he worked feverishly to get his countrymen to exercise their political power is to imagine him pushing hard on an open door. But the door did not open until he pushed.

Jefferson was not a man of contradictions so much as a person with rarely paired qualities. A true visionary, he possessed the skills of a first-class administrator. Deeply influenced by the cultivated traditions of Europe's enlightened elite, he expended his political efforts on common men. A talented amateur in botany, paleontology, and architecture, Jefferson was a consummate professional in law, public policy, and party politics. Wide-ranging in both practical and philosophical interests, he also had the tenacity to follow a project through decades to completion. Despite his vaunted tolerance, he remained deeply committed to the superiority of the white race, the male sex, and the civilized heritage of Europe. Ordinary white men were the beneficiaries of his liberating programs; blacks, women, and Indians did not engage the play of his reforming imagination.

Succeeding generations have remembered Jefferson more for his aspirations for human rights, epitomized in the words of the Declaration of Independence, than for his eight years of presidential leadership. This has been both a blessing and a curse for his reputation. A blessing, because his soaring hopes for mankind deserve a worldwide audience, but a curse—or, at least, a loss—in obscuring the impact of his executive decisions. The Jeffersonian movement that became the Democratic party under Andrew Jackson held the presidency for fifty-two of the sixty years before the Civil War, stifling at the ballot box any elite pretensions to a special calling to govern. Nearly every one of those presidents continued Jefferson's strict construction of the Constitution. Equally enduring, if more problematic, has been Jefferson's linking of high moral purpose to American foreign policy initiatives.

Coming to terms with Thomas Jefferson is not easy for Americans in the twenty-first century. His opinions about race and slavery can not be pasted over. Exploring them honestly helps us understand the conundrum of a nation dedicating itself to natural rights while legitimating human bondage. The contradictions of a slaveholder's crusade against the tyrannies of the past and the abuses of a status-conscious society will continue to puzzle us, but they have not deterred dissident groups around the globe from using Jefferson's words to fight for those ideals for more than two hundred years. In an age in which most people could not think beyond their status, their class, their region, their religion—often beyond their village—Jefferson's imaginative identification with universal freedom was extraordinary. His example enjoins us to take politics seriously, to remember that a democracy that doesn't deliberate doesn't rule, and to put our faith in free inquiry.

Epilogue

Jefferson made no effort to conceal his joy at finally leaving Washington. He loved Monticello, and he yearned to return to long-interrupted studies. The unintended consequences of a dozen disparate developments dashed his hopes for a peaceful old age, but his seventeen remaining years were extraordinarily full, even if disruptions and worries marred his dreamed-of tranquillity. There were all his projects to be reengaged, along with responding to the undertakings people brought to him, like writing histories of the American Revolution, publishing the laws of the state of Virginia, or reviewing patent legislation. He continued to receive more than a thousand letters a year, but, even so, time opened up for the twelve grandchildren who spent most of their days at Monticello. "I cannot describe the feelings of veneration, admiration, and love that existed in my heart towards him," one wrote, looking back on the times when "he walked in the garden, and would call the children to go with him," picking fruit from the highest branches or organizing races on the lawn.[1] And then there were his entrepreneurial ventures: a flour mill on the Rivanna River, a nail factory, and new cloth-making efforts.

With leisure to take stock of his accounts, Jefferson discovered that generous hospitality had left him with substantial debts. After eight years of opening the White House to judges, legislators, diplomats, friends, and foreign visitors, the cost of those cases of champagne had mounted. Despite substantial wealth in land and slaves, Jefferson saw his income drop. His farms had not prospered in his absence, and he was still struggling to pay off debts acquired during the Revolution. And through all these years he placed orders for books, art objects, and ingenious devices from his suppliers in Europe. Not until his grandson took over management of his crops did hopes for bountiful yields rise, and then they were snuffed out by the Panic of 1819 when Jefferson, like most of the country's debtors, was pushed to the brink of bankruptcy. But he didn't change his style of living; nor did the guests stop arriving at his doorstep.

The high cost of entertaining friends, acquaintances, and just about anyone with a letter of introduction continued to drain Jefferson's resources. Sometimes as many as fifty visitors spent the night at Monticello, their horses overflowing his ample stables. The longer he lived, the more a visit to Monticello became a favorite pilgrimage. A veteran of the War of 1812 left a charming vignette of his battalion's detour to salute Jefferson on their march to Detroit:

> We drew up in military array, at the base of the hill on which the great house was erected. About half way down the hill stood a very homely old man, dressed in plain Virginian cloth, his head uncovered, and his venerable locks flowing in the wind. People joked about who it could be. But how we were astonished when he advanced to our officers and introduced himself as THOMAS JEFFERSON.[2]

When he returned to Charlottesville as a private citizen, Jefferson had a chance to survey what had happened to America. The most spectacular change had been in religion; and in a perverse way it, too, had been inspired by him. Dozens of new denominations had sprung up, their preachers galvanized by a fervent drive to spread the Gospel, unrestrained by the educated upper-class clergy of the Congregationalists and Episcopalians. Jefferson and Madison had led the movement to disestablish the old Anglican Church in Virginia, but the Congregationalists of New England enjoyed their privileges well into the nineteenth century. With this powerful establishment in place, opportunity to win converts to Christianity came when Americans moved westward, leaving behind the churches, Sunday schools, choirs, and seminaries of the settled East. Revivalist preachers, with only the Bible in their saddlebags, met the religious needs of frontier families with a simple, straightforward admonition to accept the saving grace of Jesus. New denominations, such as the Methodists and Baptists, throve, as did their converts. Soon their compelling message about sin and redemption spread back from West to East, effecting a remarkable transformation of American culture as the rationalist sensibility of the Revolutionary era gave way to a new religious ardor.

Evangelical revivals turned Virginia and the rest of the South into the most pious of American regions, laying out the parameters of the twentieth century's Bible belt. Once they achieved dominance, the Presbyterians, supported by other evangelical denominations, took charge of the state's schools. The "priest-craft" that Jefferson detested had taken over from the genteel, latitudinarian Episcopalianism of his childhood. Education became more important than ever to him. Only the questioning spirit of science seemed adequate to halt a backslide to superstition and bigotry. Ministers "dread the advance of science as witches do the approach of daylight," he wrote one friend. During the Revolution, Jefferson had outlined a program of public education, which the Virginia legislature turned down. In retirement he offered it again, only to lose a second time, but not without securing approval of his plans for higher education. Here was a project that trumped all others. He sought advice from the august group of luminaries who made up his correspondents and visitors. What should be taught? Who should be hired for the first faculty? How could he block the Presbyterians, who insisted upon screening candidates for signs of Unitarianism? Jefferson's legendary perseverance won out. Within a few years he had fully developed plans for a new state university to be sited in Charlottesville, designing a rotunda whose dome could be seen from Monticello.

In the 1818 report to the Commissioners for the University of Virginia, Jefferson once more asserted his conviction that self-government required an educated citizenry. These sentiments were becoming conventional, as were Jefferson's expression of hopes for civilization, couched in an invidious comparison of his own and Native American societies:

> What, but education, has advanced us beyond the condition of our indigenous neighbors? And what chains them to their present state of barbarism and wretchedness, but a bigoted veneration for the supposed superlative wisdom of their fathers, and the preposterous idea that they are to look backward for better things, and not forward, longing, as it should seem, to return to the days of eating acorns and roots, rather than indulge in the degeneracies of civilization?

With stakes so high, it is no wonder that Jefferson wished to be remembered as the "Father of the University of Virginia," an accomplishment to be carved on his tombstone along with his authorship of the Declaration of Independence and the Virginia Statute for Religious Freedom.

Although Abigail Adams and Jefferson had exchanged letters at the time of his daughter Mary's death, the friendship between John Adams and Jefferson languished until their mutual friend Benjamin Rush effected a reconciliation. For the last thirteen years of their lives—Adams and Jefferson both died on the fiftieth anniversary of the Declaration of Independence—the two elder statesmen trolled their memories of the American revolution while registering verdicts on the country they had brought into existence. Their letters ranged freely over the fields of politics, philosophy, and literature, skirting in a gingerly fashion the causes of their becoming political opponents and rivals for office. In this famous correspondence, Adams was characteristically crusty, using his words to jab and thrust at the stupidities of the world, while Jefferson calmly steered his philosophical ship into untroubled waters. Yet he could not resist revisiting the election campaign of 1800. He unequivocally characterized their respective parties as "the enemies of reform" and its champions. The two sides, Jefferson insisted, split on the question of "the improvability of the human mind, in science, in ethics, in government." "Those who advocated reformation of institutions, *pari passu*, with the progress of science maintained that no definite limits could be assigned to that progress," he added. Still eager to define their differences, he contrasted the Federalists' use of coercive economic and political power with his party's trust in the people's capacity to act in their best interests.

Adams pushed his hobbyhorse, the inevitability of aristocracies forming in every society; he listed aristocracy's five pillars as beauty, wealth, birth, genius, and virtues. Jefferson demurred, distinguishing between artificial aristocracies based on wealth and family and the natural one arising from virtue and talent. And so they went, gently scuffing each other up along the old fault lines. When Jefferson chided Adams about the perseverance of an established church in Massachusetts, Adams came back swinging at Jefferson's use of the newfangled concept of ideology:

> '3 Vols. Of Ideology!' Pray explain to me this Neological Title! What does it mean? When Bonaparte used it I was delighted with it, upon the Common Principle of delight in every Thing we cannot understand. Does it mean Idiotism? The Science of Non Compos Menticism. The Science of lunacy. The Theory of Delerium. Or does it mean the Science of Self Love? of Amour propre?

The two men danced around the subject of slavery when it erupted into public debates in 1819. Missouri, the first state crafted from the Louisiana Purchase—Jefferson's "Empire of Liberty"—sought admission to the union as a slave state. By the 1820s, regional differences over free and slave labor had hardened into bitter animosity. Northern critics of slavery believed that they could and should do something to halt its spread. To the bill admitting Missouri to the Union, New York's James Tallmadge offered an amendment calling for the gradual emancipation of its slaves. Passed by the House, this bold act to cleanse the West of the hated institution was checked by the Senate, the South's bastion of resistance. Tallmadge called slavery a "monstrous scourge," ratcheting up the rhetoric in a debate that drew on the Founding Fathers, the Declaration of Independence, and Old Testament prophets. Then Henry Clay, who hoped to wear the Jeffersonian mantle, put together a compromise that allowed Missouri to enter the United States as a slave state but barred slavery from the rest of the states to be carved from the Louisiana Purchase. For Adams slavery was "a black cloud" hanging over the country, but he conceded that the South should solve its own problem. The Missouri Compromise marked Jefferson's descent from the high ground of opposition to slavery. He called the debate "a fire bell in the night," but he opposed the Tallmadge amendment, arguing that the dispersal of slaves through the West would have an ameliorating effect on the harshness of the system.

Jefferson kept at work on his favorite projects until the end, laying out a botanical garden for the university just months before his death. Fearful of the future of the nation now that slavery had stirred up political passions, loaded down with a battery of bank debts, feeling the frailty of age and ill health, Jefferson lost much of his resiliency. Yet ten days before his death in 1826 he could still exult in the fact that American citizens had "the free right to the unbounded exercise of reason and freedom of opinion." And then, in the very last letter he was to write, he found a metaphor to convey his deepest conviction: he rejoiced that the "general spread of the light of science has already laid open to every view the palpable truth, that the mass of mankind has not been born with saddles on their backs, nor a favored few booted and spurred, ready to ride them legitimately, by the grace of God."[3] A peculiar sentiment from a slaveholder whose estate was so encumbered as to make certain the sale of human beings who had served him all their lives. Yet it would be a grave error of historical judgment to underestimate the significance of Jefferson's successful assault on the venerable dogma of natural inequality that was based on the belief that most men and women were created to be the hewers of wood and drawers of water for the "favored few."

Notes

1: A PIVOTAL ELECTION

1. As quoted in Francis N. Stites, *John Marshall: Defender of the Constitution* (New York: HarperCollins, 1981), pp. 81–82.
2. Jefferson to Stephens Thompson, October 11, 1798, as quoted in James Lewis, "What Is to Become of Our Government?" in *The Revolution of 1800: Democracy, Race, and the New Republic*, James Horn, Jan Lewis, and Peter Onuf, eds. (Charlottesville: University of Virginia Press, 2002). I am indebted to this essay for coverage of the election of 1800.
3. As quoted in James F. Simon, *What Kind of Nation: Thomas Jefferson, John Marshall, and the Epic Struggle to Create a United States* (New York: Simon & Schuster, 2002), p. 133.
4. James M. Banner Jr., "James Ashton Bayard: Savior of the Constitution," in *Forgotten Heroes: Inspiring American Portraits from Our Leading Historians*, Susan Ware, ed. (New York: Society of American Historians, 1998), pp. 57–65.
5. Jefferson to Adams, Nov. 13, 1787; Adams to Jefferson, Dec. 6, 1787, *The Adams-Jefferson Letters: The Complete Correspondence Between Thomas Jefferson and Abigail and John Adams*, Lester J. Cappon, ed. (Chapel Hill: University of North Carolina Press, 1959), vol. I, pp. 212–13.

6. Adams to Jefferson, Dec. 6, 1787, Cappon, *Adams-Jefferson Letters*, vol. I, pp. 214–15.

7. *Jefferson: Political Writings*, Joyce Appleby and Terence Ball, eds. (Cambridge, Eng.: Cambridge University Press, 1999), p. 442.

8. Ibid., pp. 446, 448.

9. Joyce Appleby, *Capitalism and a New Social Order: The Republican Vision of the 1790s* (New York: New York University Press, 1984), pp. 54–56.

2: DEFINING HIS PRESIDENCY

1. Merrill D. Peterson, *Thomas Jefferson and the New Nation: A Biography* (New York: Oxford University Press, 1970), pp. 385–86.

2. Margaret Bayard Smith, *The First Forty Years of Washington Society*, Gaillard Hunt, ed. (New York: n.p., 1906), pp. 25–26.

3. George P. Fisher, *The Life of Benjamin Silliman* (Boston: n.p., 1866), vol. I. p. 35; *Reminiscences of James A. Hamilton* (New York, 1869), p. 42.

4. As quoted in Dumas Malone, *Jefferson the President: Second Term, 1805–1809* (Boston: Little Brown & Company, 1974), p. 40; Fifth Message to Congress.

5. Noble E. Cunningham Jr., *The Process of Government under Jefferson* (Princeton: Princeton University Press, 1978), pp. 82–85.

6. William Dunlap, *The Diary of William Dunlap* (New York: n.p., 1930), vol. II, pp. 387–88.

7. As discussed in Peterson, *Thomas Jefferson and the New Nation*, p. 730.

8. Ibid., p. 733.

9. November 29, 1813, *Correspondence between Thomas Jefferson and Pierre Samuel du Pont de Nemours*, Dumas Malone, ed. (Boston: n.p., 1930), p. 145.

3: INTERPRETING THE CONSTITUTION
IN A REPUBLICAN FASHION

1. Dumas Malone, *Jefferson the President: First Term, 1801–1805* (Boston: Little Brown & Company, 1970), p. 98.

2. Joyce Appleby, *Capitalism and a New Social Order* (New York: New York University Press, 1984), p. 64.

3. Merrill D. Peterson, *Thomas Jefferson and the New Nation: A Biography* (New York: Oxford University Press, 1970), p. 714.

4. *Jefferson: Political Writings,* Joyce Appleby and Terence Ball, eds. (Cambridge, Eng.: Cambridge University Press, 1999), pp. 396–97.

5. As quoted in James F. Simon, *What Kind of Nation: Thomas Jefferson, John Marshall, and the Epic Struggle to Create a United States* (New York: Simon & Schuster, 2002), pp. 122–23.

6. *Jefferson's Extracts from the Gospels,* Dickison W. Adams, ed. (Princeton: Princeton University Press, 1982).

7. As quoted in Malone, *Jefferson the President, First Term,* p. 126.

8. Jon Kukla, *A Wilderness So Immense: The Louisiana Purchase and the Destiny of America* (New York: Knopf, 2003).

9. As quoted in Malone, *Jefferson the President: First Term,* pp. 465–66.

10. *Continentalist* no. V (April 1782), in *The Papers of Alexander Hamilton,* Harold C. Syrett and Jacob E. Cooke, eds. (New York: Columbia University Press, 1962), vol. III, p. 76.

11. February 1, 1804, *The Writings of Thomas Jefferson,* Andrew A. Lipscomb and Albert Ellery Bergh, eds. (Washington, D.C.: n.p., 1903–4), vol. XI, pp. 2–3.

12. Adams to Jefferson, August 9, 1816, *The Adams-Jefferson Letters: The Complete Correspondence Between Thomas Jefferson and Abigail and John Adams,* Lester J. Cappon, ed. (Chapel Hill: University of North Carolina Press, 1959), vol. II, p. 487.

4: A PAINFUL REELECTION

1. William C. Dowling, *Literary Federalism in the Age of Jefferson: Joseph Dennie and the* Port Folio, *1801–1812* (Columbia, S.C.: University of South Carolina Press, 1999), p. 18.
2. *Sally Hemings and Thomas Jefferson: History, Memory and Civic Culture*, Peter Onuf and Jan Lewis, eds. (Charlottesville: University of Virginia Press, 1999).
3. Dowling, *Literary Federalism*, p. 16.
4. Ibid., pp. 17–21.
5. Jefferson to Albert Gallatin, July 12, 1803, *The Works of Thomas Jefferson*, Paul Leicester Ford, ed., (New York: The Knickerbocker Press, 1904), vol. VII, p. 252.
6. S. G. Goodrich, *Recollections of a Lifetime, or Men and Things I Have Seen: In a Series of Familiar Letters to a Friend* (New York: n.p., 1857), vol. I, p. 85.

5: CONTEST FOR THE WEST

1. As quoted in Dumas Malone, *Jefferson the President: Second Term, 1805–1809* (Boston: Little Brown & Company, 1974), p. 131.
2. *The Works of Thomas Jefferson*, Paul Leicester Ford, ed. (New York: The Knickerbocker Press, 1904), vol. I, p. 156.
3. As quoted in Malone, *Jefferson the President: Second Term*, p. 185.
4. *Voyages dans les Etats-Unis d'Amerique, fait en 1795, 1796, et 1797* (Paris: n.p., 1799), vol. I, p. xi.
5. Morris Birkbeck, *Notes on a Journey in America, from the Coast of Virginia to the Territory of Illinois*, 2nd ed. (London: n.p., 1818), pp. 35–36.

6: FOREIGN POLICY PROVES A QUAGMIRE

1. Jefferson to Adams, Nov. 13, 1787; Adams to Jefferson, Dec. 6, 1787, *The Adams-Jefferson Letters: The Complete Correspondence*

Between Thomas Jefferson and Abigail and John Adams, Lester J. Cappon, ed. (Chapel Hill: University of North Carolina Press, 1959), vol. I, pp. 168–69, 172–73; Jefferson to William Stephens Smith, Nov. 13, 1787, *The Papers of Thomas Jefferson*, Julian P. Boyd et al., eds. (Princeton: Princeton University Press, 1950–2002), vol. XII, p. 356.

2. Alexis de Tocqueville, *Democracy in America*, trans. by Harvey C. Mansfield and Delba Winthrop (Chicago: University of Chicago Press, 2000), p. 387.

3. As quoted in Dumas Malone, *Jefferson the President: Second Term, 1805–1809* (Boston: Little Brown & Company, 1974), p. 95.

4. As quoted in Merrill D. Peterson, *Thomas Jefferson and the New Nation: A Biography* (New York: Oxford University Press, 1970), p. 818.

5. Burton Spivak, *Jefferson's English Crisis: Commerce, Embargo, and the Republican Revolution* (Charlottesville: Univeristy of Virginia Press, 1979), pp. 73, 86–87.

6. As quoted in Malone, *Jefferson the President: Second Term*, p. 483.

7. March 14, 1808, *National Intelligencer*.

8. As quoted in Peterson, *Thomas Jefferson and the New Nation*, p. 913.

9. *The American Law Journal* I (1808), p. 175.

7: COMING TO TERMS WITH THOMAS JEFFERSON

1. Merrill D. Peterson, *The Jefferson Image in the American Mind* (New York: Oxford University Press, 1960), p. 246.

2. *The Works of Thomas Jefferson*, Paul Leicester Ford, ed. (New York: The Knickerbocker Press, 1904), vol. I, p. xii; Paul C. Nagel, *Descent from Glory: Four Generations of the John Adams Family* (New York: Oxford Univeristy Press, 1983), p. 353.

3. Thomas Jefferson, *Notes on the State of Virginia*, William Peden, ed. (Chapel Hill: University of North Carolina Press, 1955), pp. 162–63.

4. Jefferson to St. George Tucker, Monticello, August 28, 1797, *The Writings of Thomas Jefferson*, Andrew A. Lipscomb and Albert Ellery Bergh, eds. (Washington, D.C.: n.p., 1903–4), vol. IX, pp. 417–18.

5. Jefferson to Rufus King, July 13, 1802, in Lipscomb and Bergh, *Writings of Jefferson*, vol. X, pp. 326–27; to Dr. George Logan, May 1805, in Ford, *Works of Jefferson*, vol. VIII, p. 351.

6. Paul Finkelman, "Jefferson and Slavery: Treason Against the Hopes of the World," in *Jeffersonian Legacies*, Peter S. Onuf, ed. (Charlottesville: University Press of Virginia, 1992).

7. Jefferson to Henry Gregoire, February 25, 1809, *The Papers of Thomas Jefferson*, Julian P. Boyd et al., eds. (Princeton: Princeton University Press, 1950–2002), vol. IX, p. 15.

8. Thomas Jefferson, *Notes on the State of Virginia*, William Peden, ed. (Chapel Hill: University of North Carolina Press, 1955), pp. 138, 141, 143.

9. Ibid., pp. 162–63.

10. Jefferson to Dr. Joseph Priestley, Washington, June 19, 1802, in Lipscomb and Bergh, *Writings of Jefferson*, vol. X, pp. 324–25.

11. Jefferson to William Johnson, June 12, 1823, in Ford, *Works of Jefferson*, vol. X, pp. 226–27; Jefferson to Roger C. Weightman, Monticello, June 24, 1826, in ibid., vol. X, pp. 391–92; and Jefferson to Thomas Cooper, September 10, 1814, in Lipscomb and Bergh, *Writings of Jefferson*, vol. XII, p. 183.

12. Jefferson to James Madison, October 28, 1785, in Boyd, *Jefferson Papers*, vol. VIII, p. 632; to John Milligan, Monticello, April 6, 1816, in Lipscomb and Bergh, *Writings of Jefferson*, vol. XIV, p. 466; and to Benjamin Rush, September 23, 1800, in ibid., vol. X, p. 175.

13. Jefferson to William Short, January 3, 1793, *Life and Works of Thomas Jefferson*, Adrienne Koch and William Peden, eds. (New York: n.p., 1944), pp. 321–22.

14. As quoted in James F. Simon, *What Kind of Nation: Thomas Jefferson, John Marshall, and the Epic Struggle to Create a United States* (New York: Simon & Schuster, 2002), p. 121; William C.

Dowling, *Literary Federalism in the Age of Jefferson: Joseph Dennie and the* Port Folio, *1801–1812* (Columbia, S.C.: University of South Carolina Press, 1999), pp. 1–7.

15. *The Works of Fisher Ames,* Seth Ames, ed. (Indianapolis: Liberty Classics, 1983), vol. I, p. 161.

16. Henry Adams, *The Education of Henry Adams* (New York: n.p., 1918), p. 48.

EPILOGUE

1. As quoted in Merrill D. Peterson, *Thomas Jefferson and the New Nation: A Biography* (New York: Oxford University Press, 1970), p. 927.

2. Alfred M. Lorrain, *The Helm, the Sword, and the Cross: A Life Narrative* (Cincinnati: n.p., 1862), pp. 98–102. I am indebted to Peterson, *Jefferson and the New Nation,* for his account of Jefferson's years in retirement.

3. Jefferson to Roger C. Weightman, Monticello, June 24, 1826, *The Works of Thomas Jefferson,* Paul Leicester Ford, ed. (New York: The Knickerbocker Press, 1904), vol. X, pp. 391–92.

Milestones

1743 Born at Shadwell Plantation in Virginia.

1760–62 Studies at William and Mary College.

1764 Receives inheritance from late father, Peter Jefferson.

1767 Begins practicing law in Virginia.

1768 Is elected to Virginia House of Burgesses.

1770 Commences construction of Monticello.

1772 Marries Martha Wayles Skelton.

1772–82 Three daughters survive; two daughters and a son die in infancy.

1774 Writes "A Summary View of the Rights of British America."

1775 Is sent to Continental Congress.

1776 Drafts Declaration of Independence; is elected to Virginia House of Burgesses.

1777 Drafts Virginia Statute for Religious Freedom.

1779–81 Serves as governor of Virginia.

1782 Martha Wayles Jefferson, his wife, dies.

1783 Serves in Continental Congress.

1784–89 Serves as minister to France in Paris.

1787 Publishes *Notes on the State of Virginia*.

1790–93 Serves as first U.S. secretary of state.

1797–1801 Serves as vice president.

1801–9 Serves as president.

1803   Purchases Louisiana Territory.

1809   Returns to Monticello in retirement.

1825   University of Virginia opens.

1826   Dies, on fiftieth anniversary of Declaration of Independence.

Note on Sources

The principal collection of Jefferson's writings through 1797 is Julian P. Boyd, Charles T. Cullen, John Catanzariti, Barbara Oberg, et al., eds., *The Papers of Thomas Jefferson* (Princeton: Princeton University Press, 1950–2002). Less comprehensive, Paul Leicester Ford, ed., *The Works of Thomas Jefferson* (New York: The Knickerbocker Press, 1904) and Andrew A. Lipscomb and Albert Ellery Bergh, eds., *The Writings of Thomas Jefferson* (Washington, D.C.: n.p., 1903–4) include correspondence from his entire life. The Thomas Jefferson Memorial Foundation is now readying a Retirement Series of Jefferson's papers under the editorship of J. Jefferson Looney, which will cover the years 1809–1826.

Where the text makes clear the date of a quotation from any one of the Jefferson collections, I have not provided a footnote. Similarly, I have left uncited quotations from the well-indexed *Notes on the State of Virginia*, edited by William Peden (Chapel Hill: University of North Carolina Press, 1955), and *The Adams-Jefferson Letters: The Complete Correspondence Between Thomas Jefferson and Abigail and John Adams*, edited by Lester J. Cappon (Chapel Hill: University of North Carolina Press, 1959). Merrill D. Peterson, *Thomas Jefferson and the New Nation* (New York: Oxford University Press, 1970) remains the best one-volume biography of Jefferson. I am also indebted to Dumas Malone's two volumes on Jefferson's presidency, *Jefferson the President: First Term, 1801–1805*, and *Jefferson the President: Second Term, 1805–1809* (Boston: Little, Brown, 1970, 1974). Debts to other fine scholars of Jefferson's presidential career are noted throughout the text.

Selected Bibliography

Adair, Douglass. *Fame and the Founding Fathers: Essays.* Ed. by Trevor Colbourn. New York: Norton, 1974.

Appleby, Joyce, and Terence Ball, eds. *Jefferson: Political Writings.* Cambridge, Eng.: Cambridge University Press, 1999.

Banner, James. *To the Hartford Convention: The Federalists and the Origins of Party Politics in Massachusetts, 1789–1815.* New Haven: Yale University Press, 1970.

Cunningham, Noble E., Jr. *The Process of Government under Jefferson.* Princeton: Princeton University Press, 1978.

———. "Election of 1800." In Arthur M. Schlesinger, Jr., *History of American Presidential Elections, 1789–1969.* Vol. 1, *1789–1824.* New York: Chelsea House, 1985.

Dauer, Manning. "Election of 1804." In Arthur M. Schlesinger, Jr., *History of American Presidential Elections, 1789–1969.* Vol. 1, *1789–1824.* New York: Chelsea House, 1985.

DeConde, Alexander. *This Affair of Louisiana.* New York: Charles Scribner's Sons, 1976.

Dowling, William C. *Literary Federalism in the Age of Jefferson: Joseph Dennie and the* Port Folio, *1801–1812.* Columbia, S.C.: University of South Carolina Press, 1999.

Ellis, Richard E. *The Jeffersonian Crisis: Courts and Politics in the Young Republic.* New York: Oxford University Press, 1985.

Finkelman, Paul. *Slavery and the Founders: Race and Liberty in the Age of Jefferson*. Armonk, N.Y.: M. E. Sharpe, 1996.

Fischer, David Hacker. *The Revolution of American Conservatism: The Federalist Party in the Era of Jeffersonian Democracy*. New York: Harper & Row, 1965.

Gaustad, Edwin S. *Sworn on the Altar of God: A Religious Biography of Thomas Jefferson*. Grand Rapids, Mich.: Eerdmans, 1996.

Horn, James, Jan Lewis, and Peter Onuf, eds. *The Revolution of 1800: Democracy, Race, and the New Republic*. Charlottesville: University of Virginia Press, 2002.

Hunter, Phyllis Whitman. *Purchasing Identity in the Atlantic World: Massachusetts Merchants, 1670–1780*. Ithaca, N.Y.: Cornell University Press, 2001.

Hutson, James H., ed. *Religion and the New Republic: Faith in the Founding of America*. Lanham, Md.: Rowman and Littlefield, 2000.

John, Richard. *Spreading the News: The American Postal System from Franklin to Morse*. Cambridge, Mass.: Harvard University Press, 1995.

Levy, Leonard. *Emergence of a Free Press*. Revised and enlarged ed. of *Legacy of Suppression: Freedom of Speech and Press in Early American History* [1960]. New York: Oxford University Press, 1995.

Kerber, Linda. *Federalists in Dissent: Imagery and Ideology in Jeffersonian America*. Ithaca, N.Y.: Cornell University Press, 1970.

Majewski, John. *The House Dividing*. Baltimore: Johns Hopkins University Press, 2001.

Malone, Dumas. *Jefferson the President: First Term, 1801–1805*. Boston: Little Brown & Company, 1970.

———. *Jefferson the President: Second Term, 1805–1809*. Boston: Little Brown & Company, 1974.

McLaughlin, Jack, ed. *To His Excellency Thomas Jefferson: Letters to a President*. New York: Norton, 1991.

Newmyer, R. Kent. *John Marshall and the Heroic Age of the Supreme Court*. Baton Rouge: Louisiana State University Press, 2002.

Onuf, Peter, and Jan Lewis. *Sally Hemings and Thomas Jefferson: History, Memory and Civic Culture.* Charlottesville: University of Virginia Press, 1999.

Peterson, Merrill D. *Thomas Jefferson and the New Nation: A Biography.* New York: Oxford University Press, 1970.

Ronda, James P., ed. *Thomas Jefferson and the Changing West.* Albuquerque: University of New Mexico Press, 1987.

Risjord, Norman K. *Jefferson's America, 1760–1815.* Madison, Wisc.: Madison House, 1991.

Rosenfeld, Richard N. *American Aurora: A Democratic-Republican Returns: The Suppressed History of Our Nation's Beginnings and the Heroic Newspaper That Tried to Report It.* New York: St. Martin's Griffin, 1998.

Sheehan, Bernhard W. *Seeds of Extinction: Jeffersonian Philanthropy and the American Indians.* Chapel Hill: University of North Carolina Press, 1973.

Simon, James F. *What Kind of Nation: Thomas Jefferson, John Marshall, and the Epic Struggle to Create a United States.* New York: Simon & Schuster, 2002.

Spivak, Burton. *Jefferson's English Crisis: Commerce, Embargo, and the Republican Revolution.* Charlottesville: University of Virginia Press, 1979.

Index

ABOUT THE AUTHOR

Distinguished historian Joyce Appleby is a professor of history at UCLA. Specializing in the study of early America, Appleby has written and edited many books, including *Inheriting the Revolution: The First Generation of Americans* and *Liberalism and Republicanism in the Historical Imagination*. She has also served as president of both the Organization of American Historians and the American Historical Association. She lives in Los Angeles.